W9-DHT-373

THE MEDIEVAL LIBRARY UNDER
THE GENERAL EDITORSHIP OF
SIR ISRAEL GOLLANCZ, Litt.D., F.B.A.

The · Cell · of Self-Knowledge

seven Early English Mystical Treatises

printed · by

Henry · Pepwell

MDXXI

Edited · with · an · introduction
and · notes · by

Edmund · G · Gardner · M·A·

THE CELL OF SELF-KNOWLEDGE : SEVEN EARLY ENGLISH MYSTICAL TREATISES PRINTED BY HENRY PEPWELL IN 1521 : EDITED WITH AN INTRODUCTION AND NOTES BY EDMUND G. GARDNER, M.A.

COOPER SQUARE PUBLISHERS, INC.
NEW YORK
1966

The Frontispiece is taken from
B.M. MS. Faustina, B. VI.

" Stiamo nella cella del cognoscimento di noi ; cogno-
scendo, noi per noi non essere, e la bontà di Dio in noi ;
ricognoscendo l'essere, e ogni grazia che è posta sopra
l'essere, da lui."—*St. Catherine of Siena.*

" Tergat ergo speculum suum, mundet spiritum suum,
quisquis sitit videre Deum suum. Exterso autem speculo
et diu diligenter inspecto, incipit ei quaedam divini
luminis claritas interlucere, et immensus quidam insolitae
visionis radius oculis ejus apparere. Hoc lumen oculos
ejus irradiaverat, qui dicebat : *Signatum est super nos
lumen vultus tui, Domine ; dedisti laetitiam in corde meo.*
Ex hujus igitur luminis visione quam admiratur in se,
mirum in modum accenditur animus, et animatur ad
videndum lumen, quod est supra se."—*Richard of St.
Victor.*

Published 1966 by Cooper Square Publishers, Inc.
59 Fourth Avenue, New York, N. Y. 10003
Library of Congress Catalog Card No. 66-25702

Printed in the United States of America
by Noble Offset Printers, Inc., New York, N. Y. 10003

CONTENTS

INTRODUCTION

FROM the end of the thirteenth to the beginning of the fifteenth century may be called the golden age of mystical literature in the vernacular. In Germany, we find Mechthild of Magdeburg (*d.* 1277), Meister Eckhart (*d.* 1327), Johannes Tauler (*d.* 1361), and Heinrich Suso (*d.* 1365); in Flanders, Jan Ruysbroek (*d.* 1381); in Italy, Dante Alighieri himself (*d.* 1321), Jacopone da Todi (*d.* 1306), St. Catherine of Siena (*d.* 1380), and many lesser writers who strove, in prose or in poetry, to express the hidden things of the spirit, the secret intercourse of the human soul with the Divine, no longer in the official Latin of the Church, but in the language of their own people, " a man's own vernacular," which " is nearest to him, inasmuch as it is most closely united to him." [1] In England, the great names of Richard Rolle, the Hermit of Hampole (*d.* 1349), of Walter Hilton (*d.* 1396), and of Mother Juliana of Norwich, whose *Revelations of Divine Love* professedly date from 1373, speak for themselves.

Dante, *Convivio*, i. 12.

The seven tracts or treatises before us were published in 1521 in a little quarto volume : " Imprynted at London in Poules chyrchyarde at the sygne of the Trynyte, by Henry Pepwell. In the yere of our lorde God, M.CCCCC.XXI., the xvi. daye of Nouembre." They may, somewhat loosely speaking, be regarded as belonging to the fourteenth century, though the first and longest of them professes to be but a translation of the work of the great Augustinian mystic of an earlier age.

St. Bernard, Richard of St. Victor, and St. Bonaventura—all three very familiar figures to students of Dante's *Paradiso*—are the chief influences in the story of English mysticism. And, through the writings of his latter-day followers, Richard Rolle, Walter Hilton, and the anonymous author of the *Divine Cloud of Unknowing*, Richard of St. Victor is, perhaps, the most important of the three.

Himself either a Scot or an Irishman by birth, Richard entered the famous abbey of St. Victor, a house of Augustinian canons near Paris, some time before 1140, where he became the chief pupil of the great mystical doctor and theologian whom the later Middle Ages regarded as a second Augustine, Hugh of St. Victor. After Hugh's death (1141), Richard succeeded to his influence as a teacher, and completed his work in creating the mystical theology of the Church. His masterpiece, *De Gratia Contemplationis*, known also as *Benjamin*

Major, in five books, is a work of marvellous spiritual insight, unction, and eloquence, upon which Dante afterwards based the whole mystical psychology of the *Paradiso*.[1] In it Richard shows how the soul passes upward through the six steps of contemplation—in imagination, in reason, in understanding—gradually discarding all sensible objects of thought; until, in the sixth stage, it contemplates what is above reason, and seems to be beside reason, or even contrary to reason. He teaches that there are three qualities of contemplation, according to its intensity : *mentis dilatatio*, an enlargement of the soul's vision without exceeding the bounds of human activity ; *mentis sublevatio*, elevation of mind, in which the intellect, divinely illumined, transcends the measure of humanity, and beholds the things above itself, but does not entirely lose self-consciousness ; and *mentis alienatio*, or ecstasy, in which all memory of the present leaves the mind, and it passes into a state of divine transfiguration, in which the soul gazes upon truth without any veils of creatures, not in a mirror darkly, but in its pure simplicity. This master of the spiritual life died in 1173. Amongst the glowing souls of the great doctors and theologians in the fourth heaven, St. Thomas Aquinas

---

[1] Cf. the Letter to Can Grande (*Epist.* x. 28), where Dante, like St. Thomas Aquinas before him, refers to the *Benjamin Major* as "Richardus de Sancto Victore in libro *De Contemplatione*."

bids Dante mark the ardent spirit of " Richard who in contemplation was more than man." [1]

Benjamin, for Richard, is the type of contemplation, in accordance with the Vulgate version of Psalm lxvii. : *Ibi Benjamin adolescentulus in mentis excessu :* " There is Benjamin, a youth, in ecstasy of mind "—where the English Bible reads : " Little Benjamin their ruler." [2] At the birth of Benjamin, his mother Rachel dies : " For, when the mind of man is rapt above itself, it surpasseth all the limits of human reasoning. Elevated above itself and rapt in ecstasy, it beholdeth things in the divine light at which all human reason succumbs. What, then, is the death of Rachel, save the failing of reason ? " [3]

The treatise here printed under the title *Benjamin* is based upon a smaller work of Richard's, a kind of introduction to the *Benjamin Major*, entitled : *Benjamin Minor ;* or : *De Praeparatione animi ad Contemplationem.* It is a paraphrase of certain portions of this work, with a few additions, and large omissions. Among the portions omitted are the two passages that, almost alone among Richard's writings, are known to the general reader—or, at least, to people who do not claim to be specialists in mediæval theology. In the one, he speaks of knowledge of self as the Holy Hill, the Mountain of the Lord :—

---

[1] *Par.* x. 131, 132.
[2] Ps. lxviii. 27.
[3] *Benjamin Minor*, cap. 73.

" If the mind would fain ascend to the height of science, let its first and principal study be to know itself. Full knowledge of the rational spirit is a great and high mountain. This mountain transcends all the peaks of all mundane sciences, and looks down upon all the philosophy and all the science of the world from on high. Could Aristotle, could Plato, could the great band of philosophers ever attain to it ? " [1]

In the other, still adhering to his image of the mountain of self-knowledge, he makes his famous appeal to the Bible, as the supreme test of truth, the only sure guard that the mystic has against being deluded in his lofty speculations :—

" Even if you think that you have been taken up into that high mountain apart, even if you think that you see Christ transfigured, do not be too ready to believe anything you see in Him or hear from Him, unless Moses and Elias run to meet Him. I hold all truth in suspicion which the authority of the Scriptures does not confirm, nor do I receive Christ in His clarification unless Moses and Elias are talking with Him." [2]

---

[1] *Benjamin Minor*, cap. 75. Cf. Shelley, *The Triumph of Life :* "Their lore taught them not this : to know themselves." This passage of Richard is curiously misquoted and its meaning perverted in Hauréau, *Histoire de la Philosophie Scolastique*, i. pp. 513, 514, in the *Dictionary of National Biography*, vol. xvi., and elsewhere.

[2] *Benjamin Minor*, cap. 81.

On the other hand, the beautiful passage with which the version closes, so typical of the burning love of Christ, shown in devotion to the name of Jesus, which glows through all the writings of the school of the Hermit of Hampole, is an addition of the translator :—

" And therefore, what so thou be that covetest to come to contemplation of God, that is to say, to bring forth such a child that men clepen in the story Benjamin (that is to say, sight of God), then shalt thou use thee in this manner. Thou shalt call together thy thoughts and thy desires, and make thee of them a church, and learn thee therein for to love only this good word *Jesu*, so that all thy desires and all thy thoughts are only set for to love Jesu, and that unceasingly as it may be here ; so that thou fulfil that is said in the psalm : ' Lord, I shall bless Thee in churches ' ; that is, in thoughts and desires of the love of Jesu. And then, in this church of thoughts and desires, and in this onehead of studies and of wills, look that all thy thoughts, and all thy desires, and all thy studies, and all thy wills be only set in the love and the praising of this Lord Jesu, without forgetting, as far forth as thou mayst by grace, and as thy frailty will suffer ; evermore meeking thee to prayer and to counsel, patiently abiding the will of our Lord, unto the time that thy mind be ravished above itself, to be fed with the fair food of angels in the beholding of God and ghostly things ; so that it be fulfilled in thee that is written in the psalm : *Ibi*

Benjamin adolescentulus in mentis excessu; that is : ' There is Benjamin, the young child, in ravishing of mind.' " [1]

The text printed by Pepwell differs slightly from that of the manuscripts, of which a large number have been preserved. Among others, it is found in the Arundel MS. 286, and the Harleian MSS. 674, 1022, and 2373. It has been published from the Harl. MS. 1022 by Professor C. Horstman, who observes that " it is very old, and certainly prior to Walter Hilton." [2] It is evidently by one of the followers of Richard Rolle, dating from about the middle of the fourteenth century. External and internal evidence seems to point to its being the work of the anonymous author of the *Divine Cloud of Unknowing.*

This is not the place to tell again the wonderful story of St. Catherine of Siena (1347–1380), one of the noblest and most truly heroic women that the world has ever seen. Her life and manifold activities only touched England indirectly. The famous English captain of mercenaries, Sir John Hawkwood, was among the men of the world who, at least for a while, were won to nobler ideals by her letters and exhortations. Two of her principal disciples, Giovanni Tantucci and William Flete, both Augustinian hermits, were graduates of Cambridge ;

[1] Cf. below, pp. 32, 33.
[2] *Richard Rolle of Hampole and his Followers*, edited by C. Horstman, vol. i. pp. 162–172.

the latter, an Englishman by birth, was appointed by her on her deathbed to preside over the continuance of her work in her native city, and a vision of his, concerning the legitimacy of the claims of Urban the Sixth to the papal throne, was brought forward as one of the arguments that induced England, on the outbreak of the Great Schism in the Church (1378), to adhere to the Roman obedience for which Catherine was battling to the death. A letter which she herself addressed on the same subject to King Richard the Second has not been preserved.

About 1493, Wynkyn de Worde printed *The Lyf of saint Katherin of Senis the blessid virgin*, edited by Caxton ; which is a free translation, by an anonymous Dominican, with many omissions and the addition of certain reflections, of the *Legenda*, the great Latin biography of St. Catherine by her third confessor, Friar Raymond of Capua, the famous master-general and reformer of the order of St. Dominic (*d.* 1399). He followed this up, in 1519, by an English rendering by Brother Dane James of the Saint's mystical treatise, the *Dialogo* : " Here begynneth the Orcharde of Syon, in the whiche is conteyned the reuelacyons of seynt Katheryne of Sene, with ghostly fruytes and precyous plantes for the helthe of mannes soule." [1] This was not translated from St. Catherine's own vernacular, but from

---

[1] *Sene, Senis,* or *Seenes,* " Siena," from the Latin *Senae* (*Catharina de Senis*).

Friar Raymond's Latin version of the latter, first printed at Brescia in 1496. From the first of these two works, the *Lyf*, are selected the passages—the *Divers Doctrines devout and fruitful* — which Pepwell here presents to us ; but it seems probable that he was not borrowing directly from Caxton, as an almost verbally identical selection, with an identical title, is found in the British Museum, MS. Reg. 17 D.V., where it follows the *Divine Cloud of Unknowing*.

Margery Kempe is a much more mysterious personage. She has come down to us only in a tiny quarto of eight pages printed by Wynkyn de Worde :—

" Here begynneth a shorte treatyse of contemplacyon taught by our lorde Jhesu cryste, or taken out of the boke of Margerie kempe of Lynn."

And at the end :—

" Here endeth a shorte treatyse called Margerie kempe de Lynn. Enprynted in Fletestrete by Wynkyn de worde."

The only known copy is preserved in the University of Cambridge. It is undated, but appears to have been printed in 1501.[1] With a few insignificant variations, it is the same as was printed twenty years later by Pepwell, who merely inserts a few words like " Our Lord Jesus said unto her," or " she said," and adds that she was a

[1] Cf. E. Gordon Duff, *Hand-Lists of English Printers*, 1501-1556, i. p. 24.

devout ancress. Tanner, not very accurately, writes:
" This book contains various discourses of Christ (as it is
pretended) to certain holy women ; and, written in the
style of modern Quietists and Quakers, speaks of the
inner love of God, of perfection, et cetera." [1] No manu-
script of the work is known to exist, and absolutely no
traces can be discovered of the " Book of Margery
Kempe," out of which it is implied by the Printer that
these beautiful thoughts and sayings are taken.

There is nothing in the treatise itself to enable us to
fix its date. It is, perhaps, possible that the writer or
recipient of these revelations is the " Margeria filia
Johannis Kempe," who, between 1284 and 1298, gave
up to the prior and convent of Christ Church, Canterbury, all her rights in a piece of land with buildings and
appurtenances, " which falls to me after the decease of
my brother John, and lies in the parish of Blessed Mary of
Northgate outside the walls of the city of Canterbury." [2]
The revelations show that she was (or had been) a woman
of some wealth and social position, who had abandoned
the world to become an ancress, following the life pre-
scribed in that gem of early English devotional literature,
the *Ancren Riwle*.[3] It is clearly only a fragment of her

---

[1] *Bibliotheca Britannico-Hibernica*, p. 452.

[2] *Quietaclamium Margerie filie Johannis Kempe de domibus in
parochia de Northgate*. Brit. Mus., Add. MS. 25,109.

[3] She was, however, apparently less strictly enclosed than was
usual for an ancress.

complete book (whatever that may have been) ; but it
is enough to show that she was a worthy precursor of
that other great woman mystic of East Anglia : Juliana
of Norwich. For Margery, as for Juliana, Love is the
interpretation of revelation, and the key to the universal
mystery : [1]—

"Daughter, thou mayst no better please God, than
to think continually in His love."

"If thou wear the habergeon or the hair, fasting bread
and water, and if thou saidest every day a thousand
Pater Nosters, thou shalt not please Me so well as thou
dost when thou art in silence, and suffrest Me to speak
in thy soul."

"Daughter, if thou knew how sweet thy love is to Me,
thou wouldest never do other thing but love Me with
all thine heart."

"In nothing that thou dost or sayest, daughter, thou
mayst no better please God than believe that He loveth
thee. For, if it were possible that I might weep with
thee, I would weep with thee for the compassion that I
have of thee."

And, from the midst of her celestial contemplations,
rises up the simple, poignant cry of human suffering :
"Lord, for Thy great pain have mercy on my little pain."

We are on surer ground with the treatise that follows,

[1] Cf. G. Tyrrell, *Sixteen Revelations of Divine Love shewed to
Mother Juliana of Norwich*, Preface, p. v.

the *Song of Angels*.[1] Walter Hilton—who died on
March 24, 1396—holds a position in the religious life and
spiritual literature of England in the latter part of the
fourteenth century somewhat similar to that occupied
by Richard Rolle in its earlier years. Like the Hermit
of Hampole, he was the founder of a school, and the
works of his followers cannot always be distinguished
with certainty from his own. Like his great master in
the mystical way, Richard of St. Victor, Hilton was an
Augustinian, the head of a house of canons at Thur-
garton, near Newark. His great work, the *Scala Perfec-
tionis*, or *Ladder of Perfection*, " which expoundeth many
notable doctrines in Contemplation," was first printed
by Wynkyn de Worde in 1494, and is still widely used
for devotional reading. A shorter treatise, the *Epistle
to a Devout Man in Temporal Estate*, first printed by
Pynson in 1506, gives practical guidance to a religious
layman of wealth and social position, for the fulfilling of
the duties of his state without hindrance to his making
profit in the spiritual life. These, with the *Song of
Angels*, are the only printed works that can be assigned
to him with certainty, though many others, undoubtedly
from his pen, are to be found in manuscripts, and a complete and critical edition of Walter Hilton seems still in

---

[1] In the British Museum copy of Pepwell's volume, ff. 1–2 of
the *Epistle of Prayer* and f. 1 of the *Song of Angels* are trans-
posed.

the far future.[1] The *Song of Angels* has been twice printed since the edition of Pepwell.[2] In profoundly mystical language, tinged with the philosophy of that mysterious Neo-Platonist whom we call the pseudo-Dionysius, it tells of the wonderful " onehead," the union of the soul with God in perfect charity :—

" This onehead is verily made when the mights of the soul are reformed by grace to the dignity and the state of the first condition ; that is, when the mind is firmly established, without changing and wandering, in God and ghostly things, and when the reason is cleared from all worldly and fleshly beholdings, and from all bodily imaginations, figures, and fantasies of creatures, and is illumined by grace to behold God and ghostly things, and when the will and the affection is purified and cleansed from all fleshly, kindly, and worldly love, and is inflamed with burning love of the Holy Ghost."

But to this blessed condition none may attain perfectly here on earth. The writer goes on to speak of the mystical consolations and visitations granted to the

[1] Cf. C. T. Martin, in *Dictionary of National Biography*, vol. ix. For Hilton's alleged authorship of the *De Imitatione Christi*, see J. E. G. de Montmorency, *Thomas à Kempis, his Age and Book*, pp. 141–169.

[2] Edited by G. G. Perry, under the title *The Anehede of Godd with mannis saule*, as the work of Richard Rolle, in *English Prose Treatises of Richard Rolle de Hampole* (Early English Text Society, 1866), pp. 14–19 ; and, in two texts, by C. Horstman, *op. cit.*, vol. i. pp. 175–182.

loving soul in this life, distinguishing the feelings and
sensations that are mere delusions, from those that truly
proceed from the fire of love in the affection and the light
of knowing in the reason, and are a very anticipation of
that ineffable " onehead " in heaven.

The three remaining treatises—the *Epistle of Prayer*,
the *Epistle of Discretion in Stirrings of the Soul*, and the
Treatise of Discerning of Spirits[1]—are associated in the
manuscripts with four other works : the *Divine Cloud
of Unknowing*, the *Epistle of Privy Counsel*, a paraphrase
of the *Mystical Theology* of Dionysius entitled *Dionise
Hid Divinity*, and the similar translation or paraphrase
of the *Benjamin Minor* of Richard of St. Victor already
considered.[2] These seven treatises are all apparently by
the same hand. The *Divine Cloud of Unknowing* has
been credited to Walter Hilton, as likewise to William
Exmew, or to Maurice Chauncy, Carthusians of the
sixteenth century, whereas the manuscripts are at least
a hundred years earlier than their time ; but it seems
safer to attribute the whole series to an unknown
writer of the second part of the fourteenth century, who

---

[1] In the MSS. this is called : *A pystyll of discrecion in knowenge
of spirites ;* or : *A tretis of discrescyon of spirites.*

[2] All in Harl. MS. 674, and other MSS. The *Divine Cloud
of Unknowing,* and portions of the *Epistle, Book,* or *Treatise, of
Privy Counsel,* have been printed, in a very unsatisfactory manner,
in *The Divine Cloud with notes and a Preface by Father Augustine
Baker, O.S.B.* Edited by Henry Collins. London, 1871.

" marks a middle point between Rolle and Hilton." [1] The spiritual beauty of the three here reprinted—and, more particularly, of the *Epistle of Prayer*, with its glowing exposition of the doctrine of Pure Love—speaks for itself. They show us mysticism brought down, if I may say so, from the clouds for the practical guidance of the beginner along this difficult way. And, in the *Epistle of Discretion*, we find even a rare touch of humour ; where the counsellor " conceives suspiciously " of his correspondent's spiritual stirrings, lest " they should be conceived on the ape's manner." Like St. Catherine of Siena, though in a less degree, he has the gift of vision and the faculty of intuition combined with a homely common sense, and can illustrate his " simple meaning " with a smile.

I have borrowed a phrase from St. Catherine, " The Cell of Self-Knowledge," *la cella del cognoscimento di noi*, as the title of this little volume. Knowledge of self and purity of heart, the mystics teach, are the indispensable conditions for the highest mystical elevation. Knowledge of self, for Richard of St. Victor, is the high

[1] D. M. M'Intyre, *The Cloud of Unknowing*, in the *Expositor*, series vii. vol. 4 (1907). Dr. Rufus M. Jones, *Studies in Mystical Religion*, p. 336, regards these treatises as the work of "a school of mystics gathered about the writer of the *Hid Divinity*." Neither of these authors includes the translation of the *Benjamin Minor*, which, however, appears to me undoubtedly from the same hand as that of the *Divine Cloud*.

mountain apart upon which Christ is transfigured; for Catherine of Siena, it is the stable in which the pilgrim through time to eternity must be born again. "Wouldest thou behold Christ transfigured?" asks Richard; "ascend this mountain; learn to know thyself."[1] "Thou dost see," writes Catherine, speaking in the person of the eternal Father, "this sweet and loving Word born in a stable, while Mary was journeying; to show to you, who are travellers, that you must ever be born again in the stable of knowledge of yourselves, where you will find Him born by grace within your souls."[2] The soul is a mirror that reflects the invisible things of God, and it is by purity of heart alone that this mirror is made clear. "Therefore," writes Richard of St. Victor, "let whoso thirsts to see his God, wipe his mirror, purify his spirit. After he hath thus cleared his mirror and long diligently gazed into it, a certain clarity of divine light begins to shine through upon him, and a certain immense ray of unwonted vision to appear before his eyes. This light irradiated the eyes of him who said: *Lord, lift Thou up the light of Thy countenance upon us; Thou hast put gladness in my heart.* From the vision of this light which it sees with wonder in itself, the mind is wondrously inflamed and inspired to behold the light which is above itself."[3]

[1] *Benjamin Minor,* cap. 78.
[2] *Dialogo,* cap. 151.
[3] *Benjamin Minor,* cap. 72.

Pepwell's volume has been made the basis of the present edition of these seven treatises ; but, in each case, the text has been completely revised. The text of the *Benjamin*, the *Epistle of Prayer*, the *Epistle of Discretion*, and the *Treatise of Discerning of Spirits*, has been collated with that given by the Harleian MSS. 674 and 2373 ; and, in most cases, the readings of the manuscripts have been adopted in preference to those of the printed version. The *Katherin* has been collated with Caxton's *Lyf;* the *Margery Kempe* with Wynkyn de Worde's precious little volume in the University Library of Cambridge ; and the *Song of Angels* with the text published by Professor Horstman from the Camb. MS. Dd. v. 55. As the object of this book is not to offer a Middle English text to students, but a small contribution to mystical literature, the orthography has been completely modernised, while I have attempted to retain enough of the original language to preserve the flavour of mediæval devotion.

EDMUND G. GARDNER.

I

HERE FOLLOWETH A VERY DEVOUT TREATISE, NAMED BENJAMIN, OF THE MIGHTS AND VIRTUES OF MAN'S SOUL, AND OF THE WAY TO TRUE CONTEMPLATION, COMPILED BY A NOBLE AND FAMOUS DOCTOR, A MAN OF GREAT HOLINESS AND DEVOTION, NAMED RICHARD OF SAINT VICTOR

A TREATISE NAMED BENJAMIN

THE PROLOGUE

A GREAT clerk that men call [1] Richard of Saint
Victor, in a book that he maketh of the study of
wisdom, witnesseth and saith that two mights are in a
man's soul, given of the Father of Heaven of whom all
good cometh. The one is reason, the other is affection;
through reason we know, and through affection we feel
or love.

Of reason springeth right counsel and ghostly wits;
and of affection springeth holy desires and ordained [2]
feelings. And right as Rachel and Leah were both wives
unto Jacob, right so man's soul through light of knowing
in the reason, and sweetness of love in the affection, is
spoused unto God. By Jacob is understanden God, by
Rachel is understanden reason, by Leah is understanden
affection. Each of these wives, Rachel and Leah, took

---

[1] The MSS. have: "men clepen."
[2] So the MSS., which agrees with the Latin, *ordinati affectus*
(*Benjamin Minor*, cap. 3); Pepwell has "ardent feelings."

to them a maiden; Rachel took Bilhah, and Leah took
Zilpah.   Bilhah was a great jangler, and Zilpah was ever
drunken and thirsty.   By Bilhah is understanden imagination, the which is servant unto reason, as Bilhah was to
Rachel; by Zilpah is understanden sensuality, the which
is servant unto affection, as Zilpah was to Leah.   And
so much are these maidens needful to their ladies, that
without them all this world might serve them of nought.
For why, without imagination reason may not know,
and without sensuality affection may not feel.   And yet
imagination cryeth so inconveniently [1] in the ears of our
heart that, for ought that reason her lady may do, yet
she may not still her.   And therefore it is that oft times
when we should pray, so many divers fantasies of idle
and evil thoughts cry in our hearts, that on no wise we
may by our own mights drive them away.   And thus it is
well proved that Bilhah is a foul jangler.   And also the
sensuality is evermore so thirsty, that all that affection
her lady may feel,[2] may not yet slake her thirst.   The
drink that she desireth is the lust of fleshly, kindly, and
worldly delights,[3] of the which the more that she drinketh

1 So Pepwell, which accords with the Latin: *cum tanta impor-
tunitate.*   The MSS. read: "unconningly," *i.e.* ignorantly.

2 So Harl. MS. 674 and Pepwell; Harl. MS. 1022, ed. Horstman, reads: "forthe," *i.e.* offer.   The Latin is: "Et Zelphae
quidem sitim dominae suae copia tanta omnino extinguere non
potest" (*Benjamin Minor*, cap. 6).

3 The Latin has simply: "Vinum quod Zelpha sitit, gaudium
est voluptatis" (*ibid.*).

the more she thirsteth ; for why, for to fill the appetite of the sensuality, all this world may not suffice ; and therefore it is that oft times when we pray or think on God and ghostly things, we would fain feel sweetness of love in our affection,[1] and yet we may not, for are we so busy to feed the concupiscence of our sensuality ; for evermore it is greedily asking, and we have a fleshly compassion thereof. And thus it is well proved that Zilpah is evermore drunken and thirsty. And right as Leah conceived of Jacob and brought forth seven children, and Rachel conceived of Jacob and brought forth two children, and Bilhah conceived of Jacob and brought forth two children, and Zilpah conceived of Jacob and brought forth two children ; right so the affection conceiveth through the grace of God, and bringeth forth seven virtues ; and also the sensuality conceiveth through the grace of God, and bringeth forth two virtues ; and also the reason conceiveth through the grace of God, and bringeth forth two virtues ; and also the imagination conceiveth through the grace of God, and bringeth forth two virtues, or two beholdings. And the names of their children and of their virtues shall be known by this figure that followeth :

Husband : Jacob temporally, God spiritually. Wives to Jacob : Leah, that is to say, Affection ; Rachel, that is to say, Reason. Maid to Leah is Zilpah, that is to under-

[1] Harl. MS. 1022, ed. Horstman, reads : "in our soul."

stand, Sensuality; and Bilhah maiden to Rachel, that is to understand, Imagination.

The sons of Jacob and Leah are these seven that followeth : Reuben signifieth dread of pain; Simeon, sorrow of sins; Levi, hope of forgiveness; Judah, love of righteousness; Issachar, joy in inward sweetness; Zebulun, hatred of sin; Dinah, ordained shame.

The sons of Jacob and Zilpah, servant of Leah, are these : Gad, abstinence; Asher, patience.

The sons of Jacob and of Rachel are these : Joseph, discretion; Benjamin, contemplation.

The sons of Jacob and Bilhah, servant to Rachel, are these : Dan, sight of pain to come; and Naphtali, sight of joy to come.

In this figure it is shewed apertly of Jacob and of his wives, and their maidens, and all their children. Here it is to shew on what manner they were gotten, and in what order :—

First, it is to say of the children of Leah; for why, it is read that she first conceived. The children of Leah are nought else to understand but ordained affections or feelings in a man's soul; for why, if they were unordained, then were they not the sons of Jacob. Also the seven children of Leah are seven virtues, for virtue is nought else but an ordained and a measured feeling in a man's soul. For then is man's feeling in soul ordained when it is of that thing that it should be; then it is

measured when it is so much as it should be. These
feelings in a man's soul may be now ordained and measured, and now unordained and unmeasured ; but when
they are ordained and measured, then are they accounted
among the sons of Jacob.[1]

CAPITULUM I

HOW THE VIRTUE OF DREAD RISETH IN THE AFFECTION

THE first child that Leah conceived of Jacob was Reuben,
that is, dread ; and therefore it is written in the psalm :
" The beginning of wisdom is the dread of our Lord
God." [2]   This is the first felt virtue in a man's affection,
without the which none other may be had.   And, therefore, whoso desireth to have such a son, him behoveth
busily and oft also behold the evil that he hath done.
And he shall, on the one party, think on the greatness
of his trespass, and, on another party, the power of the
Doomsman.[3]   Of such a consideration springeth dread,
that is to say Reuben, that through right is cleped " the
son of sight." [4]   For utterly is he blind that seeth not the
pains that are to come, and dreadeth not to sin.   And

---

[1] Pepwell gives the modern equivalent, "ordinate' and "inordinate," for "ordained" and "unordained," throughout.

[2] Ps. cxi. 10 (Vulgate cx.).

[3] Pepwell adds: "and high Judge."

[4] *Filius visionis.*

well is Reuben cleped the son of sight; for when he was born, his mother cried and said: " God hath seen my meekness." [1]   And man's soul, in such a consideration of his old sins and of the power of the Doomsman, beginneth then truly to see God by feeling of dread, and also to be seen of God by rewarding of pity.

CAPITULUM II

HOW SORROW RISETH IN THE AFFECTION

WHILE Reuben waxeth, Simeon is born; for after dread it needeth greatly that sorrow come soon.   For ever the more that a man dreadeth the pain that he hath deserved, the bitterlier he sorroweth the sins that he hath done.   Leah in the birth of Simeon cried and said: " Our Lord hath heard me be had in despite." [2]   And therefore is Simeon cleped " hearing "; [3] for when a man bitterly sorroweth and despiseth his old sins, then beginneth he to be heard of God, and also for to hear the blessed sentence of God's own mouth: " Blessed be they that sorrow, for they shall be comforted." [4]   For in what hour the sinner sorroweth and turneth from his sin, he shall be safe.[5]   Thus witnesseth holy Scripture.   And

[1] Gen. xxix. 32 (*Vidit Dominus humilitatem meam*, Vulgate).
[2] Gen. xxix. 33.   [3] *Exauditio.*
[4] Matt. v. 4.   [5] Ezek. xxxiii. 14.

also by Reuben he is meeked,[1] and by Simeon he is contrite
and hath compunction of tears ; but, as witnesseth David
in the psalm : " Heart contrite and meeked God shall not
despise " ; [2] and without doubt such sorrow bringeth in
true comfort of heart.

CAPITULUM III

HOW HOPE RISETH IN THE AFFECTION

BUT, I pray thee, what comfort may be to them that truly
dread and bitterly sorrow for their old sins, ought but a
true hope of forgiveness ? the which is the third son of
Jacob, that is Levi, the which is cleped in the story " a
doing to." [3] For when the other two children, dread
and sorrow, are given of God to a man's soul, without
doubt he this third, that is hope, shall not be delayed,
but he shall be *done to* ; [4] as the story witnesseth of Levi,
that, when his two brethren, Reuben and Simeon, were
given to their mother Leah, he, this Levi, was done to.
Take heed of this word, that he was " done to " and not
given. And therefore it is said that a man shall not
presume of hope of forgiveness before the time that his
heart be meeked in dread and contrite in sorrow ; without these two, hope is presumption, and where these two

---

[1] Made humble.　　　　　　　[2] Ps. li. 17 (Vulgate l.).
[3] *Additus, vel Additio.*　　　[4] Added. Cf. Gen. xxix. 34.

are, hope is done to ; and thus after sorrow cometh soon
comfort, as David telleth in the psalm that " after the
muchness of my sorrow in my heart," he saith to our
Lord, " Thy comforts have gladded my soul." [1]   And
therefore it is that the Holy Ghost is called *Paracletus*,
that is, comforter, for oft times he vouchethsafe to comfort a sorrowful soul.

CAPITULUM IV

HOW LOVE RISETH IN THE AFFECTION

From now forth beginneth a manner of homeliness for
to grow between God and a man's soul ; and also on a
manner a kindling of love, in so much that oft times he
feeleth him not only be visited of God and comforted in
His coming, but oft times also he feeleth him filled with
an unspeakable joy.   This homeliness and this kindling
of love first felt Leah, when, after that Levi was born, she
cried with a great voice and said : " Now shall my husband
be coupled to me." [2]   The true spouse of our soul is
God, and then are we truly coupled unto Him, when we
draw near Him by hope and soothfast love.   And right as
after hope cometh love, so after Levi was Judah born, the
fourth son of Leah.   Leah in his birth cried and said :

[1] Ps. xciv. 19 (Vulgate xciii.).   [2] Gen. xxix. 34.

" Now shall I shrive to our Lord." [1]   And therefore in
the story is Judah cleped " Shrift." [2]   Also man's soul in
this degree of love offereth it clearly to God, and saith
thus : " Now shall I shrive to our Lord."   For before
this feeling of love in a man's soul, all that he doth is
done more for dread than for love ; but in this state a
man's soul feeleth God so sweet, so merciful, so good, so
courteous, so true, and so kind, so faithful, so lovely and
so homely, that he leaveth nothing in him—might, wit,
conning,[3] or will—that he offereth not it clearly, freely,
and homely unto Him.   This shrift is not only of sin,
but of the goodness of God.   Great token of love it is
when a man telleth to God that He is good.   Of this
shrift speaketh David full oft times in the psalter, when
he saith : " Make it known to God, for He is good." [4]

Lo, now have we said of four sons of Leah.   And after
this she left bearing of children till another time ; and
so man's soul weeneth that it sufficeth to it when it
feeleth that it loveth the true goods.[5]   And so it is
enough to salvation, but not to perfection.   For it
falleth to a perfect soul both to be inflamed with the fire
of love in the affection, and also to be illumined with the
light of knowing in the reason.

[1] Gen. xxix. 35 (Vulgate) : *Modo confitebor Domino.*
[2] *Confitens.*
[3] Learning.
[4] Ps. cvi. 1, cvii. 1 (cv., cvi., Vulgate).
[5] Pepwell reads : " the true goodness of God."

CAPITULUM V

HOW THE DOUBLE SIGHT OF PAIN AND JOY RISETH
IN THE IMAGINATION

THEN when Judah waxeth, that is to say, when love and desire of unseen true goods is rising and waxing in a man's affection ; then coveteth Rachel for to bear some children ; that is to say, then coveteth reason to know these things that affection feeleth ; for as it falleth to the affection for to love, so it falleth to the reason for to know. Of affection springeth ordained and measured feelings ; and of reason springeth right knowings [1] and clear understandings. And ever the more that Judah waxeth, that is to say love, so much the more desireth Rachel bearing of children, that is to say, reason studieth after knowing. But who is he that woteth not how hard it is, and nearhand impossible to a fleshly soul the which is yet rude in ghostly studies, for to rise in knowing of unseeable [2] things, and for to set the eye of contemplation in ghostly things ? For why, a soul that is yet rude and fleshly, knoweth nought but bodily things, and nothing cometh yet to the mind but only seeable [3] things.

[1] Pepwell reads : " conning."
[2] Latin *Invisibilium :* Pepwell has " unseasable."
[3] Pepwell has " feble."

And, nevertheless, yet it looketh inward as it may ; and that that it may not see yet clearly by ghostly knowing, it thinketh by imagination.

And this is the cause why Rachel had first children of her maiden than of herself. And so it is that, though all a man's soul may not yet get the light of ghostly knowing in the reason, yet it thinketh it sweet to hold the mind on God and ghostly things in the imagination. As by Rachel we understand reason, so by her maiden Bilhah we understand imagination. And, therefore, reason sheweth that it is more profitable for to think on ghostly things, in what manner so it be ; yea, if it be in kindling of our desire with some fair imagination ; than it is for to think on vanities and deceivable things of this world. And, therefore, of Bilhah were born these two : Dan and Naphtali. Dan is to say sight of pains to come ; and Naphtali, sight of joys to come. These two children are full needful and full speedful unto a working soul ; the one for to put dowr evil suggestions of sins ; and the other for to raise up our wills in working of good and in kindling of our desires. For as it falleth to Dan to put down evil suggestions of sin by sight of pains to come, so it falleth to the other brother Naphtali to raise up our wills in working of good, and in kindling of holy desires by sight of joys to come. And therefore holy men, when they are stirred to any unlawful thing, by inrising of any foul thought, as oft they set before their mind the pains that are to come ; and so they slaken their temptation in the beginning, ere it rise to any foul delight in their soul. And as oft as their devotion and their liking in God and ghostly things cease and wax cold (as oft times it befalleth in this life, for corruption of the flesh and many other skills),[1] so oft they set before their mind the joy that is to come. And so they kindle their will with holy desires, and destroy their temptation in the beginning, ere it come to any weariness or heaviness of sloth. And for that[2] with Dan we damn unlawful thoughts, therefore he is well cleped in the story " Doom." [3] And also his father Jacob said of him thus : " Dan shall deem his folk." [4] And also it is said in the story that, when Bilhah brought forth Dan, Rachel said thus : " Our Lord hath deemed me " ; [5] that is to say : " Our Lord hath evened me unto my sister Leah." And thus saith reason, when the imagination hath gotten the sight of pains to come, that our Lord hath evened her with her sister affection ; and she saith thus, for she hath the sight of pains to come in her imagination, of the which she had dread and sorrow in her feeling. And then after came Naphtali, that is to say, the sight of joys to come. And in his birth spake Rachel and said : " I am made like to

---

[1] Reasons.   [2] Because.
[3] *Judicium* (Pepwell adds : " or judgment ").
[4] Gen. xlix. 16 : " Dan shall judge his people."
[5] Gen. xxx. 6.

my sister Leah " ; [1] and therefore is Naphtali cleped in
the story " Likeness." [2]   And thus saith reason that she
is made like to her sister affection.   For there as she had
gotten hope and love of joy to come in her feeling, she
hath now gotten sight of joy to come in her imagination.
Jacob said of Naphtali that he was " a hart sent out,
giving speeches of fairhead." [3]   So it is that, when we
imagine of the joys of heaven, we say that it is fair in
heaven.   For [4] wonderfully kindleth Naphtali our souls
with holy desires, as oft as we imagine of the worthiness
and the fairhead of the joys of heaven.

CAPITULUM VI

HOW THE VIRTUES OF ABSTINENCE AND PATIENCE
RISE IN THE SENSUALITY

WHEN Leah saw that Rachel her sister made great joy
of these two bastards born of Bilhah her maiden, she
called forth her maiden Zilpah, to put to her husband
Jacob ; that she might make joy with her sister, having

[1] Gen. xxx. 8 : "Comparavit me Deus cum sorore mea, et
invalui" (Vulgate).

[2] In the Latin, "*Comparatio* vel *conversio*."

[3] Gen. xlix. 21 : "Naphtali is a hind let loose ; he giveth goodly
words" (*Nephthali cervus emissus, et dans eloquia pulchritudinis*,
Vulgate).

[4] Harl. MS. 1022, ed. Horstman, reads : "full."

other two bastards gotten of her maiden Zilpah. And thus it is seemly in man's soul for to be, that from the time that reason hath refrained the great jangling of imagination, and hath put her to be underlout [1] to God, and maketh her to bear some fruit in helping of her knowing, that right so the affection refrain the lust and the thirst of the sensuality, and make her to be underlout to God, and so to bear some fruit in helping of her feeling. But what fruit may she bear, ought but that she learn to live temperately in easy things, and patiently in uneasy things ?   These are they, the children of Zilpah, Gad and Asher : Gad is abstinence, and Asher is patience.   Gad is the sooner born child, and Asher the latter ; for first it needeth that we be attempered in ourself with discreet abstinence, and after that we bear outward disease [2] in strength of patience.   These are the children that Zilpah brought forth in sorrow ; for in abstinence and patience the sensuality is punished in the flesh ; but that that is sorrow to the sensuality turneth to much comfort and bliss to the affection.   And therefore it is that, when Gad was born, Leah cried and said : " Happily " [3] ; and therefore Gad is cleped in the story " Happiness,"

[1] *Underloute*, participle of *Underluten* (O.E. *Underlútan*), " to stoop beneath," or " submit to."   Cf. *Wycliffe's Bible*, Gen. xxxvii. 8 : "Whether thow shalt be oure kyng, oither we shal be undirloute to thi bidding ?"

[2] Discomfort.

[3] *Dixit : Feliciter.*   Gen. xxx. 11 (Vulgate).

or " Seeliness." [1]   And so it is well said that abstinence
in the sensuality is happiness [2] in the affection.   For why,
ever the less that the sensuality is delighted in her lust,
the more sweetness feeleth the affection in her love.
Also after when Asher was born, Leah said : " This shall
be for my bliss " ; [3] and therefore was Asher called in the
story " Blessed." [4]   And so it is well said that patience
in the sensuality is bliss in the affection.   For why, ever
the more disease that the sensuality suffereth, the more
blessed is the soul in the affection.   And thus by abstinence and patience we shall not only understand a
temperance in meat and drink, and suffering of outward
tribulation, but also [in] all manner of fleshly, kindly, [5]
and worldly delights, and all manner of disease, bodily
and ghostly, within or without, reasonable or unreasonable, that by any of our five wits torment or delight the
sensuality.   On this wise beareth the sensuality fruit in
help of affection, her lady.   Much peace and rest is in
that soul that neither is drunken in the lust of the sensuality, nor grutcheth [6] in the pain thereof.   The first of

---

[1] *Felicitas.*   Harl. MS. 674 adds : " whether thou wilt."

[2] The MSS. have : "selyness."

[3] Gen. xxx. 13 (Vulgate) : *Hoc pro beatitudine mea.*

[4] *Beatus.*   [5] Natural.

[6] Murmurs, complains.   Cf. Chaucer, *The Persones Tale*, ed.
Skeat, § 30 : "After bakbyting cometh grucching or murmuracion ;
and somtyme it springeth of impacience agayns God, and somtyme
agayns man.   Agayns God it is, whan a man gruccheth agayn the

these is gotten by Gad and the latter by Asher.   Here
it is to wete that first was Rachel's maiden put to the
husband or the maiden of Leah ; and this is the skill
why.   For truly, but if the jangling of the imagination,
that is to say, the in-running of vain thoughts, be first
refrained, without doubt the lust of the sensuality may
not be attempered.   And therefore who so will abstain
him from fleshly and worldly lusts, him behoveth first
seldom or never think any vain thoughts.[1]   And also
never in this life may a man perfectly despise the ease of
the flesh, and not dread the disease, but if he have before
busily beholden the meeds and the torments that are to
come.   But here it is to wete how that, with these four
sons of these two maidens, the city of our conscience is
kept wonderfully from all temptations.   For all temptation either it riseth within by thought, or else without by
some of our five wits.   But within shall Dan deem and
damn evil thoughts by sight of pain ; and without shall
Gad put against [2] false delights by use of abstinence.
Dan waketh [3] within, and Gad without ; and also their
other two brethren helpen them full much : Naphtali
maketh peace within with Dan, and Asher biddeth Gad
have no dread of his enemies.   Dan feareth the heart

peynes of helle, or agayns poverte, or los of catel, or agayn reyn
or tempest ; or elles gruccheth that shrewes han prosperitee, or
elles for that goode men han adversitee."

[1] Pepwell adds : " at the least willingly."
[2] Pepwell reads : '' put down."   [3] Watches.

with ugsomeness of hell, and Naphtali cherisheth it with
behighting [1] of heavenly bliss.   Also Asher helpeth his
brother without, so that, through them both, the wall of
the city is not broken.   Gad holdeth out ease, and Asher
pursueth disease.   Asher soon deceiveth his enemy, when
he bringeth to mind the patience of his father [2] and the
behighting of Naphtali, and thus oft times ever the more
enemies he hath, the more matter he hath of overcoming.
And therefore it is that, when he hath overcome his
enemies (that is to say, the adversities of this world),
soon he turneth him to his brother Gad to help to destroy
his enemies.   And without fail, from that he be come,
soon they turn the back, and flee.   The enemies of Gad
are fleshly delights ; but truly, from the time that a man
have patience in the pain of his abstinence, false delights
find no woning stead [3] in him.

CAPITULUM VII

HOW JOY OF INWARD SWEETNESS RISETH IN THE AFFECTION

Thus when the enemy fleeth and the city is peased, [4] then
beginneth a man to prove what the high peace of God is

[1] Promises.   Latin : *fovet promissis.*
[2] A curious mistranslation : "Sed Aser hosti suo facile illudit,
dum partem quam tuetur, alta patientiae rupe munitam conspicit"
(*Benjamin Minor*, cap. 33).   [3] Dwelling-place.
[4] Pacified.   Harl. MS. 1022, ed. Horstman, reads : "the cite
of conscience is made pesebule."

that passeth man's wit.   And therefore it is that Leah
left bearing of children unto this time that Gad and
Asher were born of Zilpah, her maiden.   For truly, but
if it be so that a man have refrained the lust and the pain
of his five wits in his sensuality by abstinence and patience,
he shall never feel inward sweetness and true joy in God
and ghostly things in the affection.   This is that Issachar,
the fifth son of Leah, the which in the story is cleped
" Meed." [1] [And well is this joy of inward sweetness
cleped " meed "]; [2] for this joy is the taste of heavenly
bliss, the which is the endless meed of a devout soul,
beginning here.   Leah, in the birth of this child, said :
" God hath given me meed, for that I have given my
maiden to my husband in bearing of children." [3] And
so it is good that we make our sensuality bear fruit in
abstaining it from all manner of fleshly, kindly, and
worldly delight, and in fruitful suffering of all fleshly
and worldly disease ; therefore our Lord of His great
mercy giveth us joy unspeakable and inward sweetness in
our affection, in earnest [4] of the sovereign joy and meed
of the kingdom of heaven.   Jacob said of Issachar that
he was " a strong ass dwelling between the terms." [5]

[1] *Merces.*
[2] So Harl. MS. 674 ; omitted in Harl. MS. 1022 and by Pepwell.
[3] Gen. xxx. 18.
[4] The MSS. read : " erles."
[5] Gen. xlix. 14 : " Issachar asinus fortis accubans inter terminos "
(Vulgate).

And so it is that a man in this state, and that feeleth the
earnest of everlasting joy in his affection, is as " an ass,
strong and dwelling between the terms " ; because that,
be he never so filled in soul of ghostly gladness and joy in
God, yet, for corruption of the flesh in this deadly life, him
behoveth bear the charge of the deadly body, as hunger,
thirst, and cold, sleep, and many other diseases ; for the
which he is likened to an ass as in body ; but as in soul he
is strong for to destroy all the passions and the lusts of
the flesh by patience and abstinence in the sensuality,
and by abundance of ghostly joy and sweetness in the
affection.   And also a soul in this state is dwelling between the terms of deadly life and undeadly life.   He
that dwelleth between the terms hath nearhand forsaken
deadliness, but not fully, and hath nearhand gotten undeadliness, but not fully ; for whiles that him needeth
the goods of this world, as meat and drink and clothing,
as it falleth to each man that liveth, yet his one foot is in
this deadly life ; and for great abundance of ghostly joy
and sweetness that he feeleth in God, not seldom but oft,
he hath his other foot in the undeadly life.   Thus I trow
that saint Paul felt, when he said this word of great
desire : " Who shall deliver me from this deadly body ? " [1]
And when he said thus : " I covet to be loosed and to be
with Christ." [2]   And thus doth the soul that feeleth
Issachar in his affection, that is to say, the joy of inward

[1] Rom. vii. 24.   [2] Phil. i. 23.

sweetness, the which is understanden by Issachar. It enforceth it to forsake this wretched life, but it may not; it coveteth to enter the blessed life, but it may not; it doth that it may, and yet it dwelleth between the terms.

CAPITULUM VIII

HOW PERFECT HATRED OF SIN RISETH IN THE AFFECTION

AND therefore it is that after Issachar Zebulun is born, that is to say, hatred of sin. And here it is to wete why that hatred of sin is never perfectly felt in a man's affection, ere the time that ghostly joy of inward sweetness be felt in the affection, and this is the skill: for ere this time was never the true cause of hatred felt in the affection. For the feeling of ghostly joy teacheth a man what sin harmeth the soul. And all after that the harm in the soul is felt much or little, thereafter is the hatred measured, more or less, unto the harming. But when a soul, by the grace of God and long travail, is come to feeling of ghostly joy in God, then it feeleth that sin hath been the cause of the delaying thereof. And also when he feeleth that he may not alway last in the feeling of that ghostly joy, for the corruption of the flesh, of the which corruption sin is the cause; then he riseth with a strong feeling of hatred against all sin and all kind of sin.

This feeling taught David us to have, where he saith in
the psalm : " Be ye wroth and will ye not sin " ; [1] that is
thus to mean : Be ye wroth with the sin, but not with
the kind.[2] For kind stirreth to the deed, but not to sin.
And here it is to wete that this wrath and this hatred is
not contrary to charity, but charity teacheth how it shall
be had both in a man's self and in his even Christian ; [3]
for a man should [not] hate sin [so that he destroy his
kind, but so that he destroy the sin and the appetite of
sin] in his kind. And, as against our even Christian, we
ought to hate sin in him, and to love him ; and of this
hatred speaketh David in the psalm, where he saith thus :
" With perfect hatred I hated them." [4] And in another
psalm he saith that " he had in hatred all wicked ways." [5]
Thus it is well proved that, ere Zebulun was born, Judah
and Issachar were both born. For but if a man have had
charity and ghostly joy in his feeling first, he may in no
wise feel this perfect hatred of sin in his affection. For
Judah, that is to say, charity, teacheth us how we shall
hate sin in ourself and in our brethren ; and Issachar,
that is to say, ghostly feeling of joy in God, teacheth us

[1] Ps. iv. 5. Harl. MS. 674 has : " *Wraththes and willeth not
synne,* or thus : *Beeth wrothe and synnith not.*"

[2] Human nature in our fellow-man.

[3] Fellow-Christian. The words in square brackets are omitted
in Harl. MS. 674.

[4] Ps. cxxxix. (Vulgate cxxxviii.) 21.

[5] Ps. cxix. (Vulgate cxviii.) 104.

why we shall hate sin in ourself and in our brethren.
Judah biddeth us hate sin and love the kind ; and Issachar
biddeth us destroy the sin and save the kind ; and thus
it falleth for to be that the kind may be made strong in
God and in ghostly things by perfect hatred and destroying of sin.   And therefore is Zebulun cleped in the story
" a dwelling stead of strength." [1]   And Leah said in his
birth : " My husband shall now dwell with me " ; [2] and
so it is that God, that is the true husband of our soul, is
dwelling in that soul, strengthening it in the affection
with ghostly joy and sweetness in His love, that travaileth
busily to destroy sin in himself and in others by perfect
hatred of the sin and all the kind of sin.   And thus it is
said how Zebulun is born.

CAPITULUM IX

HOW ORDAINED SHAME RISETH AND GROWETH IN
THE AFFECTION

But though all that a soul through grace feel in it perfect hatred of sin, whether it may yet live without sin ?
Nay, sikerly ; [3] and therefore let no man presume of
himself, when the Apostle saith thus : " If we say that we

---

[1] *Habitaculum fortitudinis.*   [2] Gen. xxx. 20.
[3] Assuredly.   Pepwell sometimes modernises this word, but not
invariably.

have no sin, we deceive ourself, and soothfastness is not in us." [1]　And also saint Austin saith that he dare well say that there is no man living without sin. [2]　And I pray thee, who is he that sinneth not in ignorance ?　Yea, and oft times it falleth that God suffereth those men to fall full grievously by the which He hath ordained other men's errors to be righted, that they may learn by their own falling how merciful they shall be in amending of others.　And for that oft times men fall grievously in those same sins that they most hate, therefore, after hatred of sin, springeth ordained shame in a man's soul ; and so it is that after Zebulun was Dinah born.　As by Zebulun hatred of sin, so by Dinah is understanden ordained shame of sin.　But wete thou well : he that felt never Zebulun, felt never yet Dinah.　Evil men have a manner of shame, but it is not this ordained shame.　For why, if they had perfect shame of sin, they should not so customably do it with will and advisement ; [3] but they shame more with a foul cloth on their body, than with a foul thought in their soul.　But what so thou be that weenest that thou hast gotten Dinah, think whether thee would shame as much if a foul thought were in thine heart, as thee would if thou

[1] I John i. 8.

[2] Cf. St. Augustine's various writings against the Pelagians, *e.g.* Epist. clvii. (*Opera*, ed. Migne, tom. ii. coll. 374 *et seq.*), *Ad Hilarium.*

[3] Deliberate intention.

were made to stand naked before the king and all his royalme; and sikerly else wete it thou right well that thou hast not yet gotten ordained shame in thy feeling, if so be that thou have less shame with thy foul heart than with thy foul body, and if thou think more shame with thy foul body in the sight of men than with thy foul heart in the sight of the King of heaven and of all His angels and holy saints in heaven.

Lo, it is now said of the seven children of Leah, by the which are understanden seven manner of affections in a man's soul, the which may be now ordained and now unordained, now measured and now unmeasured; but when they are ordained and measured, then are they virtues; and when they are unordained and unmeasured, then are they vices.   Thus behoveth a man have children [1] that they be not only ordained, but also measured.   Then are they ordained when they are of that thing that they should be, and then are they unordained when they are of that thing that they should not be; and then are they measured when they are as much as they should be, and then are they unmeasured when they are more than they should be.   For why, overmuch dread bringeth in despair, and overmuch sorrow casteth a man in to bitterness and heaviness of kind,[2] for the which he is unable to receive ghostly comfort.   And overmuch hope is presumption, and outrageous love is but flattering and

---

[1] *Warnes* in the MSS.   [2] Disposition.

faging,[1] and outrageous gladness is dissolution and wantonness, and untempered hatred of sin is woodness.[2] And on this manner, they are unordained and unmeasured, and thus are they turned in to vices, and then lose they the name of virtues, and may not be accounted amongst the sons of Jacob, that is to say, God : for by Jacob is understanden God, as it is shewed in the figure before.

CAPITULUM X

HOW DISCRETION AND CONTEMPLATION RISE IN THE REASON

THUS it seemeth that the virtue of discretion needeth to be had, with the which all others may be governed ; for without it all virtues are turned in to vices. This is Joseph, that is the late born child, but yet his father loveth him more than them all. For why, without discretion may neither goodness be gotten nor kept, and therefore no wonder though that virtue be singularly loved, without which no virtue may be had nor governed. But what wonder though this virtue be late gotten, when we may not win to the perfection of discretion without much custom and many travails of these other affections coming before ? For first behoveth us to be used in each

---

[1] Coaxing, beguiling.   Harl. MS. 674 reads : " glosing."
[2] Madness.

virtue by itself, and get the proof of them all serely,[1] ere
we may have full knowing of them all, or else can deem
sufficiently of them all.   And when we use us busily in
these feelings and beholdings before said, oft times we
fall and oft times we rise.   Then, by our oft falling, may
we learn how much wariness us behoveth have in the
getting and keeping of these virtues.   And thus sometime, by long use, a soul is led into full discretion, and
then it may joy in the birth of Joseph.   And before this
virtue be conceived in a man's soul, all that these other
virtues do, it is without discretion.   And therefore, in as
much as a man presumeth and enforceth him in any
of these feelings beforesaid, over his might and out of
measure, in so much the fouler he falleth and faileth of
his purpose.   And therefore it is that, after them all
and last, is Dinah born ; for often, after a foul fall and a
failing, cometh soon shame.   And thus after many fallings
and failings, and shames following, a man learneth by the
proof that there is nothing better than to be ruled after
counsel, the which is the readiest getting of discretion.
For why, he that doth all things with counsel, he shall
never forthink [2] it ; for better is a sly man than a strong
man ; yea, and better is list than lither strength,[3] and a

---

[1] In particular.   Pepwell has : "surely."   [2] Regret.
[3] Better is art than evil strength.   A proverbial expression.
Cf. *Layamons Brut*, 17210 (ed. Madden, ii. p. 297); *Ancren
Riwle* (ed. Morton), p. 268 (where it is rendered : "Skilful pru-
dence is better than rude force").   Cf. Prov. xxi. 22.

sly man speaketh of victories.   And here is the open skill
why that neither Leah nor Zilpah nor Bilhah might bear
such a child, but only Rachel ; for, as it is said before,
that of reason springeth right counsel, the which is
very discretion, understanden by Joseph, the first son of
Rachel ; and then at the first bring we forth Joseph in our
reason when all that we are stirred to do, we do it with
counsel.   This Joseph shall not only know what sins we
are most stirred unto, but also he shall know the weakness
of our kind, and after that either asketh, so shall he do
remedy, and seek counsel at wiser than he, and do after
them, or else he is not Joseph, Jacob's son born of Rachel.
And also by this foresaid [1] Joseph a man is not only
learned to eschew the deceits of his enemies, but also oft
a man is led by him to the perfect knowing of himself ;
and all after that a man knoweth himself, thereafter he
profiteth in the knowing of God, of whom he is the image
and the likeness.   And therefore it is that after Joseph
is Benjamin born.   For as by Joseph discretion, so by
Benjamin we understand contemplation.   And both are
they born of one mother, and gotten of one father.   For
through the grace of God lightening our reason, come we
to the perfect knowing of ourself and of God, that is
to say, after that it may be in this life.   But long after
Joseph is Benjamin born.   For why, truly but if it so be
that we use us busily and long in ghostly travails, with

[1] The MSS. have : "ilke."

the which we are learned to know ourself, we may not
be raised in to the knowing and contemplation of God.
He doth for nought that lifteth up his eye to the sight
of God, that is not yet able to see himself.   For first I
would that a man learned him to know the unseeable [1]
things of his own spirit, ere he presume to know the unseeable things of the spirit of God ; and he that knoweth
not yet himself and weeneth that he hath gotten somedeal knowing of the unseeable things of God, I doubt it
not but that he is deceived ; and therefore I rede that a
man seek first busily for to know himself, the which is
made to the image and the likeness of God as in soul.
And wete thou well that he that desireth for to see God,
him behoveth to cleanse his soul, the which is as a mirror
in the which all things are clearly seen, when it is clean ;
and when the mirror is foul, then mayst thou see nothing
clearly therein ; and right so it is of thy soul, when it
is foul, neither thou knowest thyself nor God.   As when
the candle brenneth, thou mayst then see the self candle [2]
by the light thereof, and other things also ; right so,
when thy soul brenneth in the love of God, that is, when
thou feelest continually thine heart desire after the love
of God, then, by the light of His grace that He sendeth
in thy reason, thou mayst see both thine own unworthi-

[1] *Invisibilia.*
[2] So Pepwell and Harl. MS. 674. Harl. MS. 1022, ed. Horstman,
reads: " see thiself and the candell.

ness and His great goodness. And therefore cleanse thy
mirror and proffer thy candle to the fire; and then,
when thy mirror is cleansed and thy candle brenning,
and it so be that thou wittily behold thereto, then beginneth there a manner of clarity of the light of God
for to shine in thy soul, and a manner of sunbeam that is
ghostly to appear before thy ghostly sight, through the
which the eye of thy soul is opened to behold God and
godly things, heaven and heavenly things, and all manner
of ghostly things. But this sight is but by times, when
God will vouchsafe for to give it to a working [1] soul, the
whiles it is in the battle of this deadly life; but after
this life it shall be everlasting. This light shone in the
soul of David, when he said thus in the psalm: " Lord,
the light of Thy face is marked upon us; Thou hast
given gladness within mine heart." [2]   The light of God's
face is the shining of His grace, that reformeth in us His
image that hath been disfigured with the darkness of sin;
and therefore a soul that brenneth in desire of His sight,[3]
if it hope for to have that that it desireth, wete it well it
hath conceived Benjamin. And, therefore, what is more
healfull [4] than the sweetness of this sight, or what softer
thing may be felt? Sikerly, none; and that woteth
Rachel full well. For why, reason saith that, in comparison of this sweetness, all other sweetness is sorrow,

[1] Pepwell reads: "waking."   [2] Ps. iv. 6-7.
[3] Harl. MS. 674 reads: " light."   [4] Salutary.

and bitter as gall before honey. Nevertheless, yet may a man never come to such a grace by his own slight.[1] For why, it is the gift of God without desert of man. But without doubt, though it be not the desert of man, yet no man may take such grace without great study and brenning desires coming before; and that woteth Rachel full well, and therefore she multiplieth her study, and whetteth her desires, seeking desire upon desire;[2] so that at the last, in great abundance of brenning desires and sorrow of the delaying of her desire, Benjamin is born, and his mother Rachel dieth;[3] for why, in what time that a soul is ravished above itself by abundance of desires and a great multitude of love, so that it is inflamed with the light of the Godhead, sikerly then dieth all man's reason.

And therefore, what so thou be that covetest to come to contemplation of God, that is to say, to bring forth such a child that men clepen in the story Benjamin (that is to say, sight of God), then shalt thou use thee in this manner. Thou shalt call together thy thoughts and thy desires, and make thee of them a church, and learn thee therein for to love only this good word *Jesu*, so that all thy desires and all thy thoughts are only set for to love Jesu, and that unceasingly as it may be here; so

[1] Skill.

[2] So Pepwell. Harl. MS. 674 reads: "each desire on desire." Harl. MS. 1022, ed. Horstman, has: "hekand desire unto desire."

[3] Gen. xxxv. 18.

that thou fulfill that is said in the psalm : " Lord, I shall bless Thee in churches " ; [1] that is, in thoughts and desires of the love of Jesu.   And then, in this church of thoughts and desires, and in this onehead of studies and of wills, look that all thy thoughts, and all thy desires, and all thy studies, and all thy wills be only set in the love and the praising of this Lord Jesu, without forgetting, as far forth as thou mayst by grace, and as thy frailty will suffer ; evermore meeking thee to prayer and to counsel, patiently abiding the will of our Lord, unto the time that thy mind be ravished above itself, to be fed with the fair food of angels in the beholding of God and ghostly things : [2] so that it be fulfilled in thee that is written in the psalm : *Ibi Benjamin adolescentulus in mentis excessu ;* [3] that is : "There is Benjamin, the young child, in ravishing of mind."   The grace of Jesu keep thee evermore.[4]   Amen.

[1] Ps. xxvi. (Vulgate xxv.) 12.

[2] So Harl. MSS. 1022 and 2373 ; Pepwell and Harl. MS. 674 read : "godly."

[3] Ps. lxviii. 27 (Vulgate lxvii. 28).

[4] So Harl. MS. 2373 ; omitted in Harl. MS. 674. Pepwell has instead : "To the which us bring our blessed Benjamin, Christ Jesu, Amen." Harl. MS. 1022 ends : "Jesu, Jesu, Mercy, Jesu, grant Mercy, Jesu." The whole of this concluding paragraph, which is an addition of the translator, differs considerably in Pepwell.

DEO GRATIAS

II

HERE FOLLOWETH DIVERS DOCTRINES DE-
VOUT AND FRUITFUL, TAKEN OUT OF THE
LIFE OF THAT GLORIOUS VIRGIN AND SPOUSE
OF OUR LORD, SAINT KATHERIN OF SEENES.
AND FIRST THOSE WHICH OUR LORD TAUGHT
AND SHEWED TO HERSELF, AND SITH THOSE
WHICH SHE TAUGHT AND SHEWED UNTO
OTHERS

Here followeth Divers Doctrines Devout and Fruitful, taken out of the Life of that Glorious Virgin and Spouse of Our Lord, Saint Katherin of Seenes. And first those which Our Lord Taught and Shewed to Herself, and sith those which she Taught and Shewed unto Others

THE first doctrine of our Lord is this :
"Knowest thou not, daughter, who thou art and who I am ? If thou know well these two words, thou art and shalt be blessed. Thou art she that art nought ; and I am He that am ought.[1] If thou have the very knowledge of these two things in thy soul, thy ghostly enemy shall never deceive thee, but thou shalt eschew graciously all his malice ;[2] and thou shalt never consent to any thing that is against My commandments and precepts, but all grace, all truth, and all charity thou shalt win without any hardness."

The second doctrine of our Lord is this :
"Think on Me, and I shall think on thee."

---

[1] So Pepwell and MS. Reg. 17 D.V. ; Caxton has : "Thou art she that art not, and I am he that am" ; which is nearer to the Latin.

[2] Caxton reads : "escape gracyously all his snares."

In declaring of which doctrine she was wont to say that:

" A soul which is verily united to God perceiveth not, seeth not, nor loveth not herself, nor none other soul, nor hath no mind of no creature but only on God."

And these words she expoundeth more expressly, and saith thus :

" Such a soul seeth herself, that she is very nought of herself, and knoweth perfectly that all the goodness, with all the mights of the soul, is her Maker's.   She forsaketh utterly herself and all creatures, and hideth herself fully in her Maker, our Lord Jesu ; in so much that she sendeth fully and principally all her ghostly and bodily workings in to Him ; in whom she perceiveth that she may find all goodness, and all perfection of blessedness.   And, therefore, she shall have no will to go out from such inward knowledge of Him for nothing.[1]   And of this unity of love, that is increased every day in such a soul, she is transformed in a manner in to our Lord, that she may

---

[1] Cf. Dante, *Par.* xxxiii. 100–105 :—

> " A quella luce cotal si diventa,
>   Che volgersi da lei per altro aspetto
>   È impossibil che mai si consenta ;
> Però che il ben, ch'è del volere obbietto,
>   Tutto s'accoglie in lei, e fuor di quella
>   È difettivo ciò che lì è perfetto."

"Such at that light does one become, that it were impossible ever to consent to turn from it for sight of ought else.   For the good, that is the object of the will, is wholly gathered therein, and outside it that is defective which there is perfect."

neither think, nor understand, nor love, nor have no mind but God, or else in God. For she may not see herself, nor none other creature, but only in God; nor she may not love herself, nor none other, but only in God; nor she may have no mind of herself nor of none other, but only in God, nor she may have no mind but only of her Maker. And therefore," she said, "we shall have none other business but only to think how we may please Him, unto whom we have committed all our governance both in body and soul."

The third doctrine of our Lord is this; in obtaining of virtue and ghostly strength:

"Daughter, if thou wilt get unto thee virtue and also ghostly strength,[1] thou must follow Me. Albeit that I might by My godly virtue have overcome all the power of the fiends by many manner ways of overcoming, yet, for to give you ensample by My manhood, I would not overcome him but only by taking of death upon the Cross, that ye might be taught thereby, if ye will overcome your ghostly enemies, for to take the Cross as I did; the which Cross shall be to you a great refreshing in all your temptations, if ye have mind of the pains that I suffered thereon.[2] And certainly the pains of the Cross

[1] So Pepwell: Caxton has: "yf thou wilt gete the vertu of ghostely strength."

[2] Pepwell and the MS. add: "and temptations" (Caxton: "of temptacyons"); which is clearly out of place. Cf. *Legenda*, § 104 (*Acta Sanctorum*, Aprilis, tom. iii.).

may well be called refreshing of temptations, for the more
pain ye suffer for My love, the more like ye be to Me.
And if ye be so like to Me in passion, needs ye must be
like to Me in joy.[1] Therefore for My love, daughter,
suffer patiently bitter things, and not sweet things; and
doubt in no wise, for thou shalt be strong enough for to
suffer all things patiently."

The first doctrine of this glorious virgin is this:

" A soul which is verily mete [2] to God, as much as it
hath of the love of God, so much it hath of the hate of
her own sensuality. For of the love of God naturally
cometh hate of sin, the which is done against God. The
soul, therefore, considering that the root and beginning
of sin reigneth in the sensuality, and there principally is
rooted, she is moved and stirred highly and holily with
all her mights against her own sensuality; not utterly to
destroy the root, for that may not be, as long as the soul
dwelleth in the body living in this life, but ever there
shall be left a root, namely of small venial sins. And
because she may not utterly destroy the root of sin
thus in her sensuality, she conceiveth a great displeasaunce against her sensuality, of the which displeasaunce
springeth an holy hate and a despising of the sensuality,
by the which the soul is ever well kept from her ghostly
enemies. There is nothing that keepeth the soul so

[1] 2 Cor. i. 7.
[2] Mated. Caxton has: "vertuously y-mette." Cf. *Legenda*,
§ 101: "Talis anima sic Deo conjuncta."

strong and so sure as doth such an holy hate. And that felt well the Apostle, when he said : *Cum infirmor, tunc fortior sum et potens ;*[1] that is : When I am sick and feeble in my sensuality by hate of sin, then am I stronger and mightier in my soul. Lo, of such hate cometh virtue, of such feebleness cometh strength, and of such displeasaunce cometh pleasaunce. This holy hate maketh a man meek, and to feel meek things of himself. It maketh him patient in adversity, temperate in prosperity, and setteth him in all honesty of virtue, and maketh him to be loved both of God and man. And where this holy hate is not, there is inordinate love, which is the stinking canal of all sin, and root[2] of all evil concupiscence. Do therefore," she saith, "your business to put away such inordinate love of your own self, out of your hearts, and plant therein holy hate of sin. For certain that is the right way to perfection, and amendment of all sin."

Here is a common answer which she used to say to the fiends :

" I trust in my Lord Jesu Christ, and not in myself."

Here is a rule how we shall behave us in time of temptation :

"When temptation," she saith, "ariseth in us, we should never dispute nor make questions ; for that is," she saith, " that the fiend most seeketh of us for to fall in

1 2 Cor. xii. 10.
2 " And the cause and the rote " (Caxton).

questions with him.   He trusteth so highly in the great
subtlety of his malice, that he should overcome us with
his sophistical reasons.   Therefore a soul should never
make questions, nor answer to the questions of the fiend,
but rather turn her to devout prayer, and commend her
to our Lord that she consent not to his subtle de-
mands ;   for by virtue of devout prayer, and steadfast
faith, we may overcome all the subtle temptations of the
fiend."

Here is a good conceit of this holy maid to eschew the
temptations of the fiend :

"It happeneth," she said, "that otherwhile[1] the
devout fervour of a soul loving our Lord Jesu, either by
some certain sin, or else by some new subtle temptations
of the fiend, waxeth dull and slow, and otherwhile it is
brought to very coldness ;[2] in so much that some unwitty
folks, considering that they be destitute from the ghostly

[1] Sometimes.
[2] Caxton has: "It happed she sayde that other whyle deuoute
feruour of a sowle *leuyng* oure lorde Jhesu other by somme certeyne
synne, or ellys by newe sotyll temptacyons of the fende wexyth
dull and slowe, and other whyle it is y-brought to veray coldenesse."
Pepwell and the MS. are entirely corrupt : "It happeneth (she
sayth) that otherwhyle *a synner whiche is leuynge* our Lord Jhesu
by some certeyn synne, or ellys by some certeyn temptacyons of
the fende," &c.   The original of the passage runs thus : "Fre-
quenter enim (ut inquiebat) contingit *animae Deum amanti*, quod
fervor mentalis, vel ex divina providentia, vel ex aliquali culpa,
vel ex haustis adinventionibus inimici, tepescit, et quandoque quasi
ad frigiditatem usque deducitur" (*Legenda*, § 107).

comfort the which they were wont to have, leave [1] therefore the ghostly exercise that they were wont to use of
prayer, of meditations, of reading, of holy communications,
and of penance doing ; whereby they be made more
ready to be overcome of the fiend. For he desireth
nothing else of Christ's knights, but that they should
put away their armour by the which they were wont to
overcome their enemies. A wise knight of our Lord
Jesu should not do so. But thus, the more he feeleth [2]
himself dull and slow, or cold in devotion, the rather he
should continue in his ghostly exercise, and not for to
make them less, but rather increase them."

Here is another doctrine of this holy maid, the which
she used to say to herself in edifying of others :

" Thou vile and wretched creature, art thou worthy
any manner of comfort in this life ? Why hast thou not
mind of thy sins ? What supposest thou of thyself,
wretched sinner ? Is it not enough to thee, trowest
thou not, that thou art escaped by the mercy of our
Lord from everlasting damnation ? Therefore thou
shouldest be well apaid,[3] wretch, though thou suffer all
the pains and darkness of thy soul all the days of thy life.
Why art thou, then, heavy and sorrowful to suffer such
pains, sith by God's grace thou shalt escape endless pains

---

[1] So Caxton ; Pepwell has : " leaving."

[2] Caxton has : " seeth " ; the Latin text : *quantumcumque videat seu sentiat.*

[3] Requited.

with Christ Jesu without any doubt, and be comforted endlessly, if thou bear these pains patiently. Whether hast thou chosen to serve our Lord only for the comfort that thou mayst have of Him in this life ? Nay, but for the comfort that thou shalt have of Him in the bliss of heaven. Therefore arise up now, and cease never of thy ghostly exercise that thou hast used, but rather increase to them more."

Here is an answer by the which she had a final victory of the fiend, after long threats of intolerable pains :

" I have chosen pain for my refreshing, and therefore it is not hard to me to suffer them, but rather delectable for the love of my Saviour, as long as it pleaseth His Majesty that I shall suffer them."

Here is a doctrine of the said virgin, how we should use the grace of our Lord :

" Who so could use the grace of our Lord, he should ever have the victory of all things that falleth to him. For as often," she said, " as any new thing falleth to a man, be it of prosperity or adversity, he should think in himself thus : Of this will I win somewhat. For he that can do so, shall soon be rich in virtue."

Here followeth notable doctrines of this holy maid, taken of her sermon which she made to her disciples before her passing, and the first was this :

" What so ever he be that cometh to the service of God, if he will have God truly, it is needful to him that he make his heart naked from all sensible love, not only of certain persons but of every creature what that ever he be, and then he should stretch up his soul to our Lord and our Maker, simply, with all the desire of his heart. For an heart may not wholly be given to God, but if it be free from all other love, open and simple without doubleness." And so she affirmed of herself, that it was her principal labour and business from her young age unto that time, ever for to come to that perfection. Also she said that she knew well that to such a state of perfection, in the which all the heart is given to God, a soul may not come perfectly without meditation of devout prayer, and that the prayer be grounded in meekness, and that it come not forth and proceed by any trust of any manner of virtue of him that prayeth, but alway he should know himself to be right nought. For she said that that was ever her business, to give herself to the exercise of prayer, so for to win the continual habit of prayer ; for she did see well that by prayer all virtues are increased, and made mighty and strong ; and, without prayer, they wax feeble and defail.[1] Wherefore she induced her disciples that they should busy them to prayer perseverauntly ; and therefore she told them of two manner of prayers :[2] Vocal and Mental. Vocal

---

[1] So the MS. ; Pepwell reads : "were feble and fayle" ; and Caxton : "wexed feble and defayled."

[2] Caxton reads : "prayng" (praying).

prayers, she said, should be kept certain hours in the night and in the day ordained by holy Church; but mental prayer should ever be had, in act or in habit of the soul. Also she said that, by the light of quick faith, she saw clearly and conceived in her soul that what that ever befell to her, or to any others, all cometh from God, not for hate but for great love that He hath to His creatures; and by [1] this quick faith she conceived in herself a love and a readiness to obey as well to the precepts of her sovereigns,[2] as to the commandments of God, ever thinking that their precepts should come from God, either for need of herself, or else for increase of virtue in her soul. Also she said, for to get and purchase purity of soul, it were right necessary that a man kept himself from all manner of judgments of his [neighbour, and from all idle speaking of his][3] neighbour's deeds; for in every creature we should behold only the will of God. And therefore she said that in no wise men should deem [4] creatures; that is, neither despise them by their doom [5] nor condemn them, all be it that they see them do open sin before them; but rather they should have compassion on them and pray for them, and despise them not, nor condemn

[1] So Caxton: Pepwell and MS. have: "in."

[2] Latin, *Praelatorum suorum* (*i.e.* of her ecclesiastical superiors), *Legenda*, § 361.

[3] Omitted in Pepwell and in MS.

[4] Judge. Cf. above, p. 14.

[5] Judgment.

them. Also she said that she had great hope and trust in God's providence ; for, she said, she knew well [1] by experience that the Divine providence was and is a passing great thing, for it wanteth never to them that hopeth in it.

[1] "Also she sayd that she hadde alwaye grete hope and truste in Goddes prouydence, and to this same truste she enduced her dysciples seyng unto theym that she founde and knewe" (Caxton).

DEO GRATIAS

III

HERE BEGINNETH A SHORT TREATISE OF
CONTEMPLATION TAUGHT BY OUR LORD
JESU CHRIST, OR TAKEN OUT OF THE BOOK
OF MARGERY KEMPE, ANCRESS OF LYNN

HERE BEGINNETH A SHORT TREATISE OF CONTEMPLATION
TAUGHT BY OUR LORD JESU CHRIST, OR TAKEN OUT OF
THE BOOK OF MARGERY KEMPE, ANCRESS OF LYNN

SHE desired many times that her head might be
smitten off with an axe upon a block for the love of
our Lord Jesu. Then said our Lord Jesu in her mind:
"I thank thee, daughter, that thou wouldest die for My
love; for as often as thou thinkest so, thou shalt have the
same meed in heaven, as if thou suffredest the same death,
and yet there shall no man slay thee.

"I assure thee in thy mind, if it were possible for
Me to suffer pain again, as I have done before, Me were
lever to suffer as much pain as ever I did for thy soul
alone, rather than thou shouldest depart from Me ever-
lastingly.

"Daughter, thou mayst no better please God, than
to think continually in His love."

Then she asked our Lord Jesu Christ, how she should
best love Him. And our Lord said: "Have mind of thy
wickedness, and think on My goodness.

" Daughter, if thou wear the habergeon or the hair,[1] fasting bread and water, and if thou saidest every day a thousand Pater Nosters, thou shalt [2] not please Me so well as thou dost when thou art in silence, and suffrest Me to speak in thy soul.

" Daughter, for to bid many beads, it is good to them that can not better do, and yet it is not perfect.[3] But it is a good way toward perfection. For I tell thee, daughter, they that be great fasters, and great doers of penance, they would that it should be holden the best life.[4] And they that give them unto many devotions,

---

[1] The habergeon or the hair-shirt, the former term being applied to an instrument of penance as well as to a piece of armour. Cf. Chaucer, *The Persones Tale* (ed. Skeat, § 97) : " Thanne shaltow understonde, that bodily peyne stant in disciplyne or techinge, by word or by wrytinge, or in ensample. Also in weringe of heyres or of stamin, or of haubergeons on hir naked flesh, for Cristes sake, and swiche manere penances. But war thee wel that swiche manere penances on thy flesh ne make nat thyn herte bitter or angry or anoyed of thy-self ; for bettre is to caste awey thyn heyre, than for to caste away the sikernesse of Jesu Crist. And therfore seith seint Paul : ' Clothe yow, as they that been chosen of God, in herte of misericorde, debonairetee, suffraunce, and swich manere of clothinge' ; of whiche Jesu Crist is more apayed than of heyres, or haubergeons, or hauberkes."

[2] Wynkyn de Worde has : "sholde."

[3] Wynkyn de Worde reads : " profyte."

[4] Cf. St. Catherine of Siena, Letter to William Flete (ed. Gigli, 124) : " There are some who give themselves perfectly to chastising their body, doing very great and bitter penance, in order that the sensuality may not rebel against the reason. They have set all their desire more in mortifying the body than in slaying their own

they would have that the best life. And those that give
much almesse, they would that it were holden the best
life. And I have often told thee, daughter, that thinking,
weeping, and high contemplation is the best life in earth,
and thou shalt have more merit in heaven for one year
thinking in thy mind than for an hundred year of praying
with thy mouth; and yet thou wilt not believe Me, for
thou wilt bid many beads.[1]

"Daughter, if thou knew how sweet thy love is to Me,
thou wouldest never do other thing but love Me with all
thine heart.

"Daughter, if thou wilt be high with Me in heaven,
keep Me alway in thy mind as much as thou mayst, and
forget not Me at thy meat; but think alway that I sit
in thine heart and know every thought that is therein,
both good and bad.

"Daughter, I have suffered many pains for thy love;
therefore thou hast great cause to love Me right well,
for I have bought thy love full dear."

"Dear Lord," she said, "I pray Thee, let me never
have other joy in earth, but mourning and weeping for

will. These are fed at the table of penance, and are good and
perfect; but unless they have great humility, and compel themselves to consider the will of God and not that of men, they oft
times mar their perfection by making themselves judges of those
who are not going by the same way that they are going."

[1] Perhaps, simply, "say many prayers"—without any special
reference to the rosary.

Thy love ; for me thinketh, Lord, though I were in hell, if I might weep there and mourn for Thy love as I do here, hell should not noye[1] me, but it should be a manner of heaven.   For Thy love putteth away all manner of dread of our ghostly enemy ; for I had lever be there, as long as Thou wouldest, and please Thee, than to be in this world and displease Thee ; therefore, good Lord, as Thou wilt, so may[2] it be."

She had great wonder that our Lord would become man, and suffer so grievous pains, for her that was so unkind a creature to Him.   And then, with great weeping, she asked our Lord Jesu how she might best please Him ; and He answered to her soul, saying : " Daughter, have mind of thy wickedness, and think on My goodness." Then she prayed many times and often these words : " Lord, for Thy great goodness, have mercy on my great wickedness, as certainly as I was never so wicked as Thou art good, nor never may be though I would ; for Thou art so good, that Thou mayst no better be ; and, there-fore, it is great wonder that ever any man should be departed from Thee without end."

When she saw the Crucifix, or if she saw a man had a wound, or a beast, or if a man beat a child before her, or smote a horse or another beast with a whip, if she might see it or hear it, she thought she saw our Lord beaten or wounded, like as she saw in the man or in the beast.

---

[1] Annoy.   [2] Wynkyn de Worde has : " mote."

The more she increased in love and in devotion, the more she increased in sorrow and contrition, in lowliness [1] and meekness, and in holy dread of our Lord Jesu, and in knowledge of her own frailty. So that if she saw any creature be punished or sharply chastised, she would think that she had been more worthy to be chastised than that creature was, for her unkindness against God. Then would she weep for her own sin, and for compassion of that creature.

Our Lord said to her : " In nothing that thou dost or sayest, daughter, thou mayst no better please God than believe that He loveth thee. For, if it were possible that I might weep with thee, I would weep with thee for the compassion that I have of thee."

Our merciful Lord Jesu Christ drew this creature unto His love, and to the mind of His passion, that she might not endure to behold a leper, or another sick man, specially if he had any wounds appearing on him. So she wept as if she had seen our Lord Jesu with His wounds bleeding ; and so she did, in the sight of the soul ; for, through the beholding of the sick man, her mind was all ravished in to our Lord Jesu, that she had great mourning and sorrowing that she might not kiss the leper when she met them in the way, for the love of our Lord : which was all contrary to her disposition in the years of her youth and prosperity, for then she abhorred them most.

[1] Wynkyn de Worde has: " lownesse."

Our Lord said : " Daughter, thou hast desired in thy mind to have many priests in the town of Lynn, that might sing and read night and day for to serve Me, worship Me, and praise Me, and thank Me for the goodness that I have done to thee in earth ; and therefore, daughter, I promise thee that thou shalt have meed and reward in heaven for the good wills and good desires, as if thou haddest done them in deed.

" Daughter, thou shalt have as great meed and as great reward with Me in heaven, for thy good service and thy good deeds that thou hast done in thy mind, as if thou haddest done the same with thy bodily wits without-forth.[1]

" And, daughter, I thank thee for the charity that thou hast to all lecherous men and women ; for thou prayest for them and weepest for them many a tear, desiring that I should deliver them out of sin, and be as gracious to them as I was to Mary Magdalene, that they might have as much grace to love Me as Mary Magdalene had ; and with this condition thou wouldest that everich[2] of them should have twenty pounds a year to love and praise Me ; and, daughter, this great charity which thou hast to them in thy prayer pleaseth Me right well.   And,

[1] With-out-forth=outwardly. Cf. Chaucer, *The Persones Tale* (ed. Skeat, § 10) : " And with-inne the hertes of folk shal be the bytinge conscience, and with-oute-forth shal be the world al brenninge."

[2] Everyche=each one.

daughter, also I thank thee for the charity which thou hast in thy prayer, when thou prayest for all Jews and Saracens, and all heathen people that they should come to Christian faith, that My name might be magnified in them. Furthermore, daughter, I thank thee for the general charity that thou hast to all people that be now in this world, and to all those that are to come unto the world's end; that thou wouldest be hacked as small as flesh to the pot for their love, so that I would by thy death save them all from damnation, if it pleased Me. And, therefore, daughter, for all these good wills and desires, thou shalt have full meed and reward in heaven, believe it right well and doubt never a deal."

She said : " Good Lord, I would be laid naked upon an hurdle for Thy love, all men to wonder on me and to cast filth and dirt on me, and be drawn from town to town every day my life time, if Thou were pleased thereby, and no man's soul hindered. Thy will be fulfilled and not mine."

" Daughter," He said, " as oftentimes as thou sayest or thinkest : *Worshipped be all the holy places in Jerusalem, where Christ suffered bitter pain and passion in :* thou shalt have the same pardon as if thou were there with thy bodily presence, both to thyself and to all those that thou wilt give to.[1]

[1] According to the legend, certain " indulgences," to be gained by all who visited the Holy Places at Jerusalem, were first granted

" The same pardon that was granted thee aforetime, it was confirmed on Saint Nicholas day, that is to say, playne[1] remission ; and it is not only granted to thee, but also to all those that believe, and to all those that shall believe unto the world's end, that God loveth thee, and shall thank God for thee.   If they will forsake their sin, and be in full will no more to turn again thereto, but be sorry and heavy for that they have done, and will do due penance therefore, they shall have the same pardon that is granted to thyself ; and that is all the pardon that is in Jerusalem,[2] as was granted thee when thou were at Rafnys." [3]

That day that she suffered no tribulation for our Lord's sake, she was not merry nor glad, as that day when she suffered tribulation.

Our Lord Jesus said unto her : " Patience is more worth than miracles doing.   Daughter, it is more pleasure to Me that thou suffer despites, scorns, shames, reproofs,

by Pope St. Sylvester at the petition of Constantine and St. Helena. There seems no evidence as to the real date at which these special indulgences were instituted.   Cf. Amort, *De origine, progressu, valore, ac fructu Indulgentiarum*, Augsburg, 1735, pars i. pp. **217** *et seq.*

[1] Plenary.

[2] All the indulgences attached to the Holy Places.

[3] Probably Racheness in the parish of South Acre, where "there was a leper hospital, with church or chapel dedicated to St. Bartholomew, of early foundation" (*Victoria History of the County of Norfolk*, ii. p. 450).

wrongs, and diseases, than if thine head were stricken off three times a day every day in seven year."

" Lord," she said, " for Thy great pain have mercy on my little pain."

When she was in great trouble, our Lord said : " Daughter, I must needs comfort thee, for now thou hast the right way to heaven. By this way came I and all My disciples ; for now thou shalt know the better what sorrow and shame I suffered for thy love, and thou shalt have the more compassion when thou thinkest on My passion."

" O my dear worthy Lord," said she, " these graces Thou shouldest shew to religious men and to priests."

Our Lord said to her again : " Nay, nay, daughter, for that I love best that they love not, and that is shames, reproofs, scorns, and despites of the people ; and therefore they shall not have this grace ; for, daughter, he that dreadeth the shames of this world may not per- fectly love God."

Here endeth a short treatise of a devout ancress called Margery Kempe of Lynn

IV

HERE FOLLOWETH A DEVOUT TREATISE
COMPILED BY MASTER WALTER HYLTON
OF THE SONG OF ANGELS

DEAR brother in Christ, I have understanding by
thine own speech, and also by telling of another
man, that thou yearnest and desirest greatly for to have
more knowledge and understanding than thou hast of
angel's song and heavenly sound; what it is, and on what
wise it is perceived and felt in a man's soul, and how a
man may be siker that it is true and not feigned; and how
it is made by the presence of the good angel, and not by
the inputting of the evil angel. These things thou wouldest
wete of me; but, soothly, I cannot tell thee for a surety
the soothfastness of this matter; nevertheless somewhat,
as me thinketh, I shall shew thee in a short word.

Wete thou well that the end and the sovereignty of
perfection standeth in very onehead [1] of God and of a
man's soul by perfect charity. This onehead, then, is
verily made when the mights of the soul are reformed by
grace to the dignity and the state of the first condition ;
that is, when the mind is stabled sadly, [2] without changing

---

[1] In true union.   [2] Established firmly.

and vagation,[1] in God and ghostly things, and when the reason is cleared from all worldly and fleshly beholdings, and from all bodily imaginations, figures, and fantasies of creatures, and is illumined by grace to behold God and ghostly things, and when the will and the affection is purified and cleansed from all fleshly, kindly, and worldly love, and is inflamed with brenning love of the Holy Ghost. This wonderful onehead may not be fulfilled [2] perfectly, continually, and wholly in this life, for the corruption of the flesh, but only in the bliss of heaven. Nevertheless, the nearer that a soul in this present life may come to this onehead, the more perfect it is. For the more that it is reformed by grace to the image and the likeness of its Creator here on this wise ; the more joy and bliss shall it have in heaven. Our Lord God is an endless being without changing, almighty without failing, sovereign wisdom, light, soothness without error or darkness ; sovereign goodness, love, peace, and sweetness. Then the more that a soul is united, fastened, conformed, and joined to our Lord, the more stable and mighty it is, the more wise and clear, good and peaceable, loving and more virtuous it is, and so it is more perfect. For a soul that hath by the grace of Jesu, and long travail of bodily and ghostly exercise, overcome and destroyed

[1] Wandering.
[2] So Horstman.   Pepwell reads : " With this wonderful onehede ne may none be fulfilled."

concupiscences, and passions, and unskilful stirrings[1]
within itself, and without in the sensuality, and is clothed
all in virtues, as in meekness and mildness, in patience and
softness, in ghostly strength and righteousness, in con-
tinence, in wisdom, in truth, hope and charity ; then it
is made perfect, as it may be in this life. Much comfort
it receiveth of our Lord, not only inwardly in its own
privy substance,[2] by virtue of the onehead to our Lord
that lieth in knowing and loving of God, in light and
ghostly brenning of Him, in transforming of the soul in
to the Godhead ; but also many other comforts, savours,
sweetnesses, and wonderful feelings on sere[3] or sundry
manners, after that our Lord vouchethsafe to visit His
creatures here in earth, and after that the soul profiteth
and waxeth in charity. Some soul, by virtue of charity
that God giveth it, is so cleansed, that all creatures, and
all that he heareth, or seeth, or feeleth by any of his wits,
turneth him to comfort and gladness ; and the sensuality
receiveth new savour and sweetness in all creatures.[4]
And right as beforetime the likings in the sensuality were

[1] Unreasonable impulses.

[2] Secret nature. Cf. Mother Juliana, *Revelations of Divine
Love*, xiv. cap. 46 : " And our kindly substance is now blessed-
fully in God."

[3] Divers.

[4] Cf. *De Imitatione Christi*, ii. 4 : " If thine heart were right,
then every creature would be a mirror of life, and a book of holy
doctrine. There is no creature so small and vile, as not to repre-
sent the goodness of God."

fleshly, vain, and vicious, for the pain of the original sin ;
right so now they are made ghostly and clean, without
bitterness and biting of conscience. And this is the
goodness of our Lord, that sith the soul is punished in the
sensuality, and the flesh is partner of the pain, that afterward the soul be comforted in the sensuality, and the flesh
be fellow of joy and comfort with the soul, not fleshly,
but ghostly, as he was fellow in tribulation and pain.
This is the freedom and the lordship, the dignity, and
the worship that a man [1] hath over all creatures, the
which dignity he may so recover by grace here, that every
creature savour to him as it is. And that is, when by
grace he seeth, he heareth, he feeleth only God in all
creatures. On this manner of wise a soul is made ghostly
in the sensuality by abundance of charity, that is, in the
substance of the soul. Also, our Lord comforteth a soul
by angel's song. What that song is, it may not be de-
scribed by no bodily likeness, for it is ghostly, and above
all manner of imagination and reason. It may be felt
and perceived in a soul, but it may not be shewed.
Nevertheless, I shall speak thereof to thee as me thinketh.
When a soul is purified by the love of God, illumined by
wisdom, stabled by the might of God, then is the eye
of the soul opened to behold ghostly things, as virtues and
angels and holy souls, and heavenly things. [2] Then is

[1] Horstman reads : "a mans saule."

[2] So Horstman : Pepwell reads : "as virtues in angels and in
holy souls and in heavenly things."

the soul able because of cleanness to feel the touching, the speaking of good angels. This touching and speaking, it is ghostly and not bodily.[1] For when the soul is lifted and ravished out of the sensuality, and out of mind of any earthly things, then in great fervour of love and light (if our Lord vouchsafe) the soul may hear and feel heavenly sound, made by the presence of angels in loving of God. Not that this song of angels is the sovereign joy of the soul; but for the difference that is between a man's soul in flesh and an angel, because of uncleanness, a soul may not hear it, but by ravishing in love, and needeth for to be purified well clean, and fulfilled of much charity, or [2] it were able for to hear heavenly sound. For the sovereign and the essential joy is in the love of God by Himself and for Himself, and the secondary is in communing and beholding of angels and ghostly creatures. For right as a soul, in understanding of ghostly things, is often times touched and moved through bodily imagination by working of angels; as Ezekiel the prophet did see in bodily imagination the soothfastness of God's privities; [3] right so, in the love of God, a soul by the presence of angels is ravished out of mind of all earthly and fleshly things in to an heavenly joy, to hear angel's song and heavenly sound, after that the charity is more

[1] Pepwell omits the "not."
[2] Before.
[3] The truth of God's hidden mysteries.

or less.[1] Now, then, me thinketh that there may no soul feel verily angel's song nor heavenly sound, but he be in perfect charity ; though all that are in perfect charity have not felt it, but only that soul that is so purified in the fire of love that all earthly savour is brent out of it, and all mean letting [2] between the soul and the cleanness of angels is broken and put away from it.   Then soothly may he sing a new song, and soothly he may hear a blessed heavenly sound, and angel's song without deceit or feigning.   Our Lord woteth where that soul is that, for abundance of brenning love, is worthy to hear angel's song.   Who so then will hear angel's song, and not be deceived by feigning of himself, nor by imagination, nor by the illusion of the enemy, him behoveth for to have perfect charity ; and that is when all vain love and dread, vain joy and sorrow, is cast out of the heart, so that it love nothing but God, nor dread nothing but God, nor joyeth, nor sorroweth nothing but in God, or for God.   Who so might by the grace of God go this way, he should not err.   Nevertheless, some men are deceived by their own imagination, or by the illusion of the enemy in this manner.[3]   Some man, when he hath long travailed bodily and ghostly in destroying of sins and getting of virtues, and peradventure hath gotten by

---

[1] According to the measure of its love.
[2] All intervening hindrance.
[3] Horstman reads : " matter."

grace a somedeal [1] rest, and a clarity in conscience, anon he leaveth prayers, readings of holy scriptures, and meditations of the passion of Christ, and the mind of his wretchedness ; and, or [2] he be called of God, he gathereth his own wits by violence to seek and to behold heavenly things, or his eye be made ghostly by grace, and over-travaileth by imaginations his wits, and by indiscreet travailing turneth the brains in his head, and forbreaketh [3] the mights and the wits of the soul and of the body. And then, for feebleness of the brain, him thinketh that he heareth wonderful sounds and songs ; and that is nothing else but a fantasy, caused of troubling of the brain ; as a man that is in a frenzy, him thinketh that he heareth and seeth that none other man doth ; and all is but vanity and fantasies of the head, or else it is by working of the wicked enemy that feigneth such sounds in his hearing.

For if a man have any presumption in his fantasies and in his workings, and thereby falleth in to indiscreet imagination, as it were in a frenzy, and is not ordered nor ruled of grace, nor comforted by ghostly strength, the devil entereth in, and by his false illuminations, and by his false sounds, and by his false sweetnesses, he deceiveth a man's soul.

And of this false ground springeth errors, and heresies,

[1] A little.   [2] Before.   [3] Overtaxes.

false prophecies, presumptions, and false reasonings, blasphemings, and slanderings, and many other mischiefs. And, therefore, if thou see any man ghostly occupied fall in any of these sins and these deceits, or in frenzies, wete thou well that he never heard nor felt angel's song nor heavenly sound. For, soothly, he that heareth verily angel's song, he is made so wise that he shall never err by fantasy, nor by indiscretion, nor by no slight [1] of working of the devil.

Also, some men feel in their hearts as it were a ghostly sound, and sweet songs in divers manners ; and this is commonly good, and sometime it may turn to deceit. This sound is felt on this wise. Some man setteth the thought of his heart only in the name of Jesu, and stead-fastly holdeth it thereto, and in short time him thinketh that that name turneth him to great comfort and sweet-ness, and him thinketh that the name soundeth in his heart delectably, as it were a song ; and the virtue of this liking is so mighty, that it draweth in all the wits of the soul thereto. Who so may feel this sound and this sweetness verily in his heart, wete thou well that it is of God,[2] and, as long as he is meek, he shall not be deceived. But this is not angel's song ; but it is a song of the soul by virtue of the name and by touching of the good angel.[3]

---

[1] Craft.
[2] Horstman reads : " wete he wele. '
[3] This passage is defective in Pepwell.

For when a soul offereth him to Jesu truly and meekly,
putting all his trust and his desire in Him, and busily
keepeth Him in his mind, our Lord Jesu, when He will,
pureth [1] the affection of the soul, and filleth it, and
feedeth it with sweetness of Himself, and maketh His
name in the feeling of the soul [2] as honey, and as song,
and as any thing that is delectable ; so that it liketh the
soul evermore for to cry *Jesu, Jesu*. And not only he
hath comfort in this, but also in psalms and hymns, and
anthems of holy Church, that the heart singeth them
sweetly, devoutly, and freely, without any travail of the
soul, or bitterness in the same time,[3] and notes that holy
Church useth. This is good, and of the gift of God,
for the substance of this feeling lies in the love of Jesu,
which is fed and lightened [4] by such manner of songs.
Nevertheless, in this manner of feeling, a soul may be
deceived by vain glory ; not in that time that the affection singeth to Jesu, and loveth Jesu in sweetness of Him,
but afterward, when it ceaseth and the heart keeleth [5]
of the love of Jesu, then entereth in vain glory. Also
some man is deceived on this wise : he heareth well say

[1] MS. Dd. v. 55, ed. Horstman, has: "purges."
[2] Pepwell has : "in feeling of the sound."
[3] MS. Dd. v. 55, ed. Horstman, reads: "toune" (*i.e.* tone).
[4] Illumined.
[5] Cools down, grows cold. Also construed with "from." Cf.
Richard Rolle, *Psalter* (ed. H. R. Bramley, p. 156): "He gars
sa many kele fra godis luf."

that it is good to have Jesu in his mind, or any other good
word of God ; then he straineth his heart mightily to
that name, and by a custom he hath it nearhand alway
in his mind ; and, nevertheless, he feeleth not thereby in
his affection sweetness, nor light of knowing in his reason,
but only a naked mind of God,[1] or of Jesu, or of Mary,
or of any other good word.   Here may be deceit, not for
it is evil for to have Jesu in mind on this wise, but if he
this feeling and this mind, that is only his own working
by custom, hold it a special visitation of our Lord,[2] and
think it more than it is.   For wete thou well that a naked
mind or a naked imagination of Jesu, or of any ghostly
thing, without sweetness of love in the affection, or
without light of knowing in reason, it is but a blindness,
and a way to deceit, if a man hold it in his own sight
more than it is.   Therefore I hold it siker [3] that he be
meek in his own feeling, and hold this mind in regard
nought, till he may, by custom and using of this mind,
feel the fire of love in his affection, and the light of knowing in his reason.   Lo, I have told thee in this matter a
little, as me thinketh ; not affirming that this sufficeth,
nor that this is the soothfastness in this matter.   But if

---

[1] A mere abstract thought of God.

[2] Construe : " But if he hold this feeling and this mind (that is
only his own working by custom) to be a special visitation."

[3] Surer, safer.

thou think it otherwise, or else any other man savour by grace the contrary hereto, I leave this saying, and give stead to him ; it sufficeth to me for to live in truth [1] principally, and not in feeling.

[1] Pepwell adds : " and in faith."

EXPLICIT

V

HERE AFTER FOLLOWETH A DEVOUT TREA-
TISE CALLED THE EPISTLE OF PRAYER

GHOSTLY friend in God, as touching thine asking of
me, how thou shalt rule thine heart in the time of
thy prayer, I answer unto thee thus feebly as I can. And I
say that me thinketh that it should be full speedful unto
thee at the first beginning of thy prayer, what prayer so
ever it be, long or short, for to make it full known unto
thine heart, without any feigning, that thou shalt die at
the end of thy prayer.[1] And wete thou well that this is no
feigned thought that I tell thee, and see why ; for truly
there is no man living in this life that dare take upon him
to say the contrary : that is to say, that thou shalt live
longer than thy prayer is in doing. And, therefore, thou
mayst think it safely, and I counsel thee to do it. For,
if thou do it, thou shalt see that, what for the general
sight that thou hast of thy wretchedness, and this special
sight of the shortness of time of amendment, it shall bring
in to thine heart a very working of dread.

[1] The MSS. add : "And bot if thou spede thee the rather or
thou come to the ende of thy prayer."

And this working shalt thou feel [1] verily folden in thine heart, but if it so be (the which God forbid) that thou flatter and fage [2] thy false fleshly blind heart with leasings [3] and feigned behightings, that thou shalt longer live.[4] For though it may be sooth in thee in deed that thou shalt live longer, yet it is ever in thee a false leasing for to think it before, and for to behight [5] it to thine heart. For why, the soothfastness of this thing is only in God, and in thee is but a blind abiding of His will, without certainty of one moment, the which is as little or less than a twinkling of an eye. And, therefore, if thou wilt pray wisely as the prophet biddeth when he saith in the psalm : *Psallite sapienter ;* [6] look that thou get thee in the beginning this very working of dread. For, as the same prophet saith in another psalm : *Initium sapientiae timor Domini ;* [7] that is : " The beginning of wisdom is the dread of our Lord God." But for that there is no full sikerness standing [8] upon dread only, for fear of sinking in to over much heaviness, therefore shalt thou knit to thy first thought this other thought that followeth.

[1] Pepwell reads : " find."   [2] Coax, beguile.

[3] Falsehoods.

[4] The MSS. read : " behetynges of lenger leuyng."

[5] Promise.

[6] Ps. xlvi. 8 (Vulgate), xlvii. 7 (A.V.) : " Sing ye praises with understanding."

[7] Ps. cxi. 10 (cx. 10 Vulgate).

[8] So Pepwell ; Harl. MS. 674 reads : " Bot forthi that there is no sekir stonding."

Thou shalt think steadfastly that if thou may, through
the grace of God, distinctly pronounce the words of that
prayer, and win to the end thereof, or if thou die before
thou come to the end, so that thou do that in thee is,
that then it shall be accepted of thee unto God, as a full
aseeth [1] of all thy recklessness from the beginning of thy
life unto that moment. I mean thus : standing that thou
hast before time, after thy conning and thy conscience,
lawfully amended thee after the common ordinance of
holy Church in confession ; this short prayer, so little
as it is, shall be accepted of thee unto God for thy full
salvation, if thou then didst die, and to the great increase
of thy perfection, if thou didst live longer. This is the
goodness of God, the which, as the prophet saith, forsaketh
none that truly trusteth in Him with will of amendment ; [2]
and sith that all amendment standeth in two—that is,
in leaving of evil and doing of good—means to get these
two are none readier than the ghostly working of these
two thoughts touched before. For what reaveth from
a soul [3] more readily the affection of sinning, than doth
a true working of dread of death ? And what moveth a

---

[1] Pepwell adds in explanation : " or amends " ; *i.e.* satisfaction.
Cf. Langland, *Piers the Plowman*, B. xvii. 237 : " And if it suffice
noughte for assetz " ; and Wyclif, *Pistle on Cristemasse Day*
(Select English Works, ed. T. Arnold, ii. p. 237) : " And thus,
sith aseeth muste be maad for Adams synne."

[2] Ps. xxxiv. 22 (Vulgate xxxiii. 23).

[3] The MSS. read : " fro a lyf."

soul[1] more fervently to working of good, than doth a
certain hope in the mercy and the goodness of God, the
which is brought in by this second thought ?   For why,
the ghostly feeling of this second thought, when it is thus
truly joined to the first, shall be to thee a sure staff of
hope to hold thee by in all thy good doings.   And by
this staff thou mayst sikerly climb in to the high mount
of perfection, that is to say, to the perfect love of God ;
though all this beginning be imperfect, as thou shalt
hear after.   For, what for the general sight that thou
hast of the mercy and of the goodness of God, and this
special experience that thou feelest of His mercy and His
goodness in this acceptation of this little short service
for so long recklessness, as it were in a full aseeth of so
much recklessness (as it is said before), it may not be but
that thou shalt feel a great stirring of love unto Him that
is so good and so merciful unto thee—as the steps of thy
staff, hope, plainly sheweth unto thee in the time of thy
prayer, if thou do it duly as I have told thee before.[2]
The ghostly experience of the proof of this working
standeth all in a reverent affection that a man hath to
God in the time of his prayer, caused of this dread in the
ground of this work, and of this stirring of love, the

---

[1] The MSS. read : "a lyf."
[2] So Harl. MS. 674.   Pepwell reads : " Also the steps of thy staff
Hope plainly will shew unto thee if thou do it duly, as I have told
thee before, or not."

which is brought in by the ghostly steps of this staff hope, touched before. For why, reverence is nought else but dread and love medled together with a staff of certain hope.

Me thinketh that the proof of this working is devotion; for devotion is nought else, as saint Thomas the doctor saith, but a readiness of man's will to do those things that longeth to the service of God.[1] Each man prove in himself, for he that doth God's service in this manner, he feeleth how ready that his will is thereto. Me thinketh that saint Bernard accordeth to this working, where he saith that all things should be done swiftly and gladly. And see why: swiftly for dread, and gladly for hope, and lovely trust in His mercy. [And what more? Sikerly, I had lever have his meed that lasteth in such doing, though all he never did bodily penance in this life, but only that that is enjoined to him of holy Church, than of all the penance-doers that have been in this life from the beginning of the world unto this day without this manner of doing. I say not that the naked thinking of these two thoughts is so meedful; but that reverent affection, to the which bringing in these two thoughts are sovereign means on man's party, that is it that is so meedful as I say.[2]] And this is only it by itself, without any other

---

[1] *Summa Theologica*, II.-ii. Q. 82, A. 1: "Devotio nihil aliud esse videtur, quam voluntas quaedam prompte tradendi se ad ea, quae pertinent ad Dei famulatum."

[2] The whole passage included in square brackets is omitted in Pepwell, but is identical in the two MSS.

manner of doing (as is fasting, waking, sharp wearing, and all these other), the which only by itself pleaseth almighty God, and deserveth to have meed of Him. And it were impossible any soul to have meed of God without this, and all after the quantity of this shall stand the quantity of meed ; for whoso hath much of this, much meed shall he have, and whoso hath less of this, less meed shall he have. And all these other things, as is fasting, waking, sharp wearing, and all these other, they are needful [1] in as much as they are helply to get this, so that without this they are nought. And this without them is sometime sufficient at the full by it-self, and it is often times full worthily had and come to of full many without any of the others. All this I say for that I would by this knowing that thou charged and commended each thing after that it is : the more, " the more," and the less, " the less " ; for oft times unknowing is cause of much error. And oft times unknowing maketh men to charge more and commend more bodily exercise (as is fasting, waking, sharp wearing, and all these others) than they do ghostly exercise in virtues or in this reverent affection touched before. And, therefore, in more decla-ration of the meed and the worthiness of this reverent affection, I shall say a little more than I yet have said, so that, by such declaring, thou mayst be better learned in this working than thou yet art.

[1] So Harl. MS. 2373 ; Harl. MS. 674 reads : " medeful."

All this manner of working beforesaid of this reverent affection, when it is brought in by these two thoughts of dread and of hope coming before, may well be likened to a tree that were full of fruit ; of the which tree, dread is that party that is within in the earth, that is, the root. And hope is that party that is above the earth, that is, the body [1] with the boughs. In that that hope is certain and stable, it is the body ; in that it stirreth men to works of love, it is the boughs ; but this reverent affection is evermore the fruit, and then, evermore as long as the fruit is fastened to the tree,[2] it hath in party a green smel of the tree ; but when it hath been a certain time departed from the tree and is full ripe, then it hath lost all the taste of the tree, and is king's meat [that was before but knave's meat].[3] In this time it is that this reverent affection is so meedful as I said. And, therefore, shape thee for to depart this fruit from the tree, and for to offer it up by itself to the high King of heaven ; and then shalt thou be cleped God's own child, loving Him with a chaste love for Himself, and not for His goods.[4] I mean thus : though all that the innumerable good deeds, the which almighty God of His gracious goodness hath shewed to each soul in this life, be sufficient causes

---

[1] The trunk.
[2] Pepwell inserts : "it is but churl's meat, for."
[3] Not in Pepwell.
[4] Pepwell reads : "and for nothing else."

at the full and more, to each soul to love Him for, with all his mind, with all his wit, and with all his will; yet if it might be, that may no wise be, that a soul were as mighty, as worthy, and as witty as all the saints and angels that are in heaven gathered in one, and had never taken this worthiness of God,[1] or to whom that God had never shewed kindness in this life; yet this soul, seeing the loveliness of God in Himself, and the abundance thereof, should be ravished over his might for to love God, till the heart brast; so lovely and so liking, so good and so glorious He is in Himself.

O how wonderful a thing and how high a thing is the love of God for to speak of, of the which no man may speak perfectly to the understanding of the least party thereof, but by impossible ensamples, and passing the understanding of man! And thus it is that I mean when I say loving Him with a chaste love for Himself, and not for His goods;[2] not as if I said (though all I well said) much for His goods, but without comparison more for Himself. For, if I shall more highly speak in declaring of my meaning of the perfection and of the meed of this

---

[1] Had never received it from Him.

[2] Pure Love, or Charity, which "attains to God Himself, that it may abide in Him, not that any advantage may accrue to us from Him" (St. Thomas Aquinas, *Summa Theologica*, II.–ii. Q. 23, A. 6). For the whole doctrine of "Pure Love or Disinterested Religion," cf. F. von Hügel, *The Mystical Element of Religion*, ii. pp. 152–181.

reverent affection, I say that a soul touched in affection
by the sensible presence of God, as He is in Himself,
and in a perfect soul illumined in the reason, by the
clear beam of everlasting light, the which is God, for to
see and for to feel the loveliness [1] of God in Himself,
hath for that time and for that moment lost all the mind
of any good deed or of any kindness that ever God did
to him in this life—so that cause for to love God for
feeleth he or seeth he none in that time, other than is
God Himself.   So that though all it may be said in speaking of the common perfection, that the great goodness
and the great kindness that God hath shewed to us in
this life are high and worthy causes for to love God for ;
yet having beholding to the point and the prick of perfection (to the which I purpose to draw thee in my meaning, and in the manner of this writing), a perfect lover of
God, for dread of letting [2] of his perfection, seeketh now,
that is to say, in the point of perfection, none other cause
for to love God for, but God Himself ; so that by this
meaning I say, that chaste love is to love God for Himself
and not for His goods.   And therefore, following the rule
of mine ensample, shape thee to depart the fruit from
the tree, and for to offer it up by itself unto the King of
heaven, that thy love be chaste ; for evermore as long
as thou offrest Him this fruit green and hanging on the

[1] So both MSS. ; Pepwell reads : " blessedness."
[2] Hindering or marring.

tree, thou mayst well be likened to a woman that is not chaste, for she loveth a man more for his goods than for himself.   And see why that I liken thee thus ; for it seemeth that dread of thy death and shortness of time, with hope of forgiveness of all thy recklessness, maketh thee to be in God's service so reverent as thou art.   And if it so be, soothly then hath thy fruit a green smell of the tree ; and though all it pleaseth God in party, nevertheless, yet it pleaseth Him not perfectly, and that is for thy love is not yet chaste.

Chaste love is that when thou askest of God neither releasing of pain, nor increasing of meed, nor yet sweetness in His love in this life ; but if it be any certain time that thou covetest sweetness as for a refreshing of thy ghostly mights, that they fail not in the way ; but thou askest of God nought but Himself, and neither thou reckest nor lookest after whether thou shalt be in pain or in bliss, so that thou have Him that thou lovest—this is chaste love, this is perfect love.[1]   And therefore shape thee for to depart the fruit from the tree ; that is to say, this reverent affection from the thoughts of dread and of hope coming before ; so that thou mayst offer it ripe and chaste unto God by itself, not caused of any thing beneath Him, or medled with Him [2] (yea, though all it

[1] Cf. St. Thomas Aquinas, *Summa Theologica*, II.-ii. Q. 27, A. 3 ; and F. von Hügel, *op. cit.*, ii. p. 167.

[2] In the Divine Essence.

be the chief),[1] but only of Him, by Himself; and then it
is so meedful as I say that it is.   For it is plainly known
without any doubt unto all those that are expert in the
science of divinity and of God's love, that as often as a
man's affection is stirred unto God without mean (that
is, without messenger of any thought in special causing
that stirring), as oft it deserveth everlasting life.   And
for that that a soul that is thus disposed (that is to say,
that offreth the fruit ripe, and departed from the tree)
may innumerable times in one hour be raised in to God
suddenly without mean, therefore more than I can say it
deserveth, through the grace of God, the which is the
chief worker, to be raised in to joy.   And therefore shape
thee for to offer the fruit ripe and departed from the
tree.   Nevertheless, the fruit upon the tree, continually
offered as man's frailty will suffer, deserveth salvation;
but the fruit ripe and departed from the tree, suddenly
offered unto God without mean, that is perfection.
And here mayst thou see that the tree is good, though
all that I bid thee depart the fruit therefrom, for more
perfection; and therefore I set it in thy garden; for
I would that thou should gather the fruit thereof, and
keep it to thy Lord.   And for that that I would that
thou knew what manner of working it is that knitteth
man's soul to God, and that maketh it one with Him in

[1] So Harl. MS. 674.   I take " it " as the beatitude of man which
is God Himself.

love and accordance of will,[1] after the word of saint Paul
saying thus : *Qui adhaeret Deo unus spiritus est cum illo ;* [2]
that is to say : " Who so draweth near to God," as it is
by such a reverent affection touched before, " he is one
spirit with God." That is, though all that God and he
be two and sere [3] in kind, nevertheless yet in grace they
are so knit together that they are but one in spirit ; [4]
and all this is for onehead of love and accordance of will ;
and in this onehead is the marriage made between God
and the soul, the which shall never be broken, though all
that the heat and the fervour of this work cease for a time,
but by a deadly sin.

In the ghostly feeling of this onehead may a loving
soul both say and sing (if it list) this holy word that is
written in the book of songs in the Bible : *Dilectus meus
mihi et ego illi ;* [5] that is : " My loved unto me and I
unto Him " ; understanden that God shall be knitted
with the ghostly glue of grace on His party, and the
lovely consent in gladness of spirit on thy party.

---

[1] Cf. Dante, *Par.* xxxiii. 143-145 :—

> " Ma già volgeva il mio disiro e il velle,
> Sì come rota ch' egualmente è mossa,
> L'Amor che move il sole e l'altre stelle."

" But already my desire and will, even as a wheel that is equally
moved, were being turned by the Love that moves the sun and
the other stars."

[2] 1 Cor. vi. 17.   [3] Pepwell adds : " or sundry."

[4] So Pepwell and Harl. MS. 2373 ; Harl. MS. 674 reads : " they
ben one spirit."   [5] Cant. ii. 16.

And therefore climb up by this tree, as I said in the beginning; and when thou comest to the fruit (that is, to the reverent affection, the which ever will be in thee if thou think heartily the other two thoughts before, and fage [1] not thyself with no lie, as I said), then shalt thou take good keep [2] of that working that is made in thy soul that time, and shape thee, in as much as thou mayst through grace, for to meek thee under the height of thy God, so that thou mayst use thee in that working other times by itself, without any climbing thereto by any thought. And, sikerly, this is it the which is so meedful as I said, and ever the longer that it is kept from the tree (that is to say, from any thought), and ever the ofter that it is done suddenly, lustily, and likingly, without mean, the sweeter it smelleth, and the better it pleaseth the high King of heaven. And ever when thou feelest sweetness and comfort in thy doing, then He breaketh this fruit and giveth thee part of thine own present. And that that thou feelest is so hard, and so straitly stressing thine heart without comfort in the first beginning, that bemeaneth [3] that the greenness of the fruit hanging on the tree, or else newly pulled, setteth thy teeth on edge. Nevertheless yet it is speedful to thee. For it is no

---

[1] Harl. MS. 674 reads: "glose." Pepwell adds: "or flatter."
[2] Heed.
[3] Pepwell adds: "or betokeneth." Cf. Langland, *Piers the Plowman*, A. i. 1: "What this mountein bemeneth."

reason that thou eat the sweet kernel, but if thou crack first the hard shell and bite of the bitter bark.

Nevertheless, if it so be that thy teeth be weak (that is to say, thy ghostly mights), then it is my counsel that thou seek slights, for better is list than lither strength.[1]

Another skill there is why that I set this tree in thy garden, for to climb up thereby. For though all it be so that God may do what He will, yet, to mine understanding, it is impossible any man to attain to the perfection of this working without these two means, or else other two that are according to them coming before. And yet is the perfection of this work sudden, without any mean. And, therefore, I rede [2] thee that these be thine, not thine in propriety, for that is nought but sin,[3] but thine given graciously of God, and sent by me as a messenger though I be unworthy ; for wete thou right well that every thought that stirreth thee to the good,[4] whether it come from within by thine angel messenger, or from without by any man messenger, it is but an instrument of grace given, sent and chosen of God Himself for to work within in thy soul. And this is the skill why that I counsel thee to take these two thoughts before all others. For as man is a mingled thing of two sub-

---

1 Cf. above, p. 28 note.
2 Pepwell adds : " or counsel."
3 Of thyself thou hast nought but sin.
4 So the MSS. : Pepwell has : " to God."

stances, a bodily and a ghostly, so it needeth for to have
two sere [1] means to come by to perfection ; [2] sith it so
is that both these substances shall be oned in undeadliness
at the uprising in the last day ; so that either substance
be raised to perfection in this life, by a mean accordant
thereto. And that is dread to bodily substance, and
hope to the ghostly. And thus it is full seemly and according to be, as me thinketh ; for as there is nothing
that so soon will ravish the body from all affection of
earthly things, as will a sensible dread of the death ; so
there is nothing that so soon nor so fervently will raise
the affection of a sinner's soul, unto the love of God, as
will a certain hope of forgiveness of all his recklessness.
And therefore have I ordained thy climbing by these

[1] Pepwell changes to " divers."
[2] Cf. Dante, *De Monarchia*, iii. 16: "Man alone of beings
holds a mid-place between corruptible and incorruptible ; wherefore he is rightly likened by the philosophers to the horizon which
is between two hemispheres. For man, if considered after either
essential part, to wit soul and body, is corruptible if considered
only after the one, to wit the body, but if after the other, to wit
the soul, he is incorruptible. . . . If man, then, is a kind of mean
between corruptible and incorruptible things, since every mean
savours of the nature of the extremes, it is necessary that man
should savour of either nature. And since every nature is ordained
to a certain end, it follows that there must be a twofold end of
man, so that like as he alone amongst all beings partakes of
corruptibility and incorruptibility, so he alone amongst all beings
should be ordained for two final goals, of which the one should be
his goal as a corruptible being, and the other as an incorruptible "
(P. H. Wicksteed's translation).

two thoughts; but if it so be that thy good angel teach thee within thy ghostly conceit, or any other man, any other two that are more according to thy disposition than thee thinketh these two be, thou mayst take them, and leave these safely without any blame. Nevertheless to my conceit (till I wete more) me thinketh that these should be full helply unto thee, and not much unaccording to thy disposition, after that I feel in thee. And therefore, if thou think that they do thee good, then thank God heartily, and for God's love pray for me. Do then so, for I am a wretch, and thou wotest not how it standeth with me.

No more at this time, but God's blessing have thou and mine.

Read often, and forget it not; set thee sharply to the proof; and flee all letting and occasion of letting, in the name of our Lord Jesu Christ. AMEN.

FINIS

VI

HERE FOLLOWETH ALSO A VERY NECESSARY
EPISTLE OF DISCRETION IN STIRRINGS OF
THE SOUL

GHOSTLY friend in God, that same grace and joy
that I will to myself, will I to thee at God's will.
Thou askest me counsel of silence and of speaking, of
common dieting and of singular fasting, of dwelling in
company and only woning[1] by thyself. And thou sayest
thou art in great were[2] what thou shalt do; for, as thou
sayest, on the one party thou art greatly tarried with
speaking, with common eating, as other folk do, and with
common woning in company. And, on the other party,
thou dreadest to be straitly still,[3] singular in fasting, and
only in woning, for deeming of more holiness in thee than
thou hast,[4] and for many other perils; for oft times now
these days they are deemed for most holy, and fall in to
many perils, that most are in silence, in singular fasting,

---

[1] Pepwell modernises this throughout to "dwelling alone."
[2] Pepwell substitutes "doubt." Cf. Chaucer, *Legend of Good Women*, 2686: "Thryes doun she fil in swiche a were."
[3] Pepwell adds: "in keeping of silence."
[4] Harl. MS. 674 reads: "more holiness than thou art worthy."

95

and in only woning.   And sooth it is that they are most
holy, if grace only be the cause of that silence, of that
singular fasting, and of that only woning, the kind [1] but
suffering and only consenting; and if it be otherwise, then
that is but peril on all sides, for it is full perilous to strain
the kind to any such work of devotion, as is silence or
speaking, common dieting or singular fasting, woning in
company or in onliness. [2]   I mean, passing the course and
the common custom of kind and degree, but if it be led
thereto by grace ;   and, namely, to such works the which
in themselves are indifferent, that is to say, now good,
and now evil, now with thee, now against thee, now helping, and now letting.   For it might befall that, if thou
followed thy singular stirring, straitly straining thee to
silence, to singular fasting, or to only woning, that thou
shouldest oft times be still when time were to speak, oft
times fast when time were to eat, oft times be only when
time were to be in company.   Or if thou give thee to
speaking always when thee list, to common eating, or to
companious woning, [3] then peradventure thou shouldest
sometime speak when time [4] were to be still, sometime
eat when time were to fast, sometime be in company
when time were to be only ;   and thus mightest thou
lightly fall in to error, in great confusion, not only of
thine own soul but also of others.   And, therefore, in

---

[1] Nature.   [2] Solitude.
[3] Pepwell has : " company."   [4] Pepwell reads : " better."

eschewing of such errors, thou askest of me (as I have perceived by thy letters) two things : the first is my conceit of thee, and thy stirring; and the other is my counsel in this case, and in all such others when they come.

As to the first, I answer and I say that I dread full much in this matter and such others to put forth my rude conceit, such as it is, for two skills.[1]   And one is this : I dare not lean to my conceit, affirming it for fast and true. The other is thine inward disposition, and thine ableness that thou hast unto all these things that thou speakest of in thy letter, which be not yet so fully known unto me, as it were speedful that they were, if I should give full counsel in this case.   For it is said of the Apostle : *Nemo novit quae sunt hominis, nisi spiritus hominis qui in ipso est ;* " No man knoweth which are the privy dispositions of man, but the spirit of the same man, the which is in himself " ;[2] and, peradventure, thou knowest not yet thine own inward disposition thyself, so fully as thou shalt do hereafter, when God will let thee feel it by the proof, among many fallings and risings.   For I knew never yet no sinner that might come to the perfect knowing of himself and of his inward disposition, but if he were learned of it before in the school of God, by experience of many temptations, and by many fallings and risings ; for right as among the waves and the floods and the

---

[1] Causes.   [2] I Cor. ii. II.

storms of the sea, on the one party, and the peaceable
wind and the calms and the soft weathers of the air on
the other party, the sely [1] ship at the last attains to the
land and the haven ; right so, among the diversity of
temptations and tribulations that falleth to a soul in this
ebbing and flowing life (the which are ensampled by
the storms and the floods of the sea) on the one party,
and among the grace and the goodness of the Holy Ghost,
the manyfold visitation, sweetness and comfort of spirit
(the which are ensampled by the peaceable wind and the
soft weathers of the air) on the other party, the sely soul,
at the likeness of a ship, attaineth at the last to the land
of stableness, and to the haven of health ; the which is
the clear and the soothfast knowing of himself, and of
all his inward dispositions, through the which knowing
he sitteth quietly in himself, as a king crowned in his
royalme, mightily, wisely, and goodly governing himself
and all his thoughts and stirrings, both in body and in
soul.   Of such a man it is that the wise man saith thus :
*Beatus vir qui suffert tentationem, quoniam cum probatus
fuerit, accipiet coronam vitae, quam repromisit Deus dili-
gentibus se :* " He is a blissful man that sufferingly beareth
temptation ; for, from he have been proved, he shall take
the crown of life, the which God hath hight to all those
that love Him." [2]   The crown of life may be said on
two manners.   One for ghostly wisdom, for full discre-

----

[1] Simple.   [2] Jas. i. 12.

tion, and for perfection of virtue : these three knitted together may be cleped [1] a crown of life, the which by grace may be come to here in this life. On another manner the crown of life may be said, that it is the endless joy that each true soul shall have, after this life, in the bliss of heaven, and, sikerly, neither of these two crowns may a man take, but if he before have been well proved in suffering of noye [2] and of temptation, as this text saith : *Quoniam cum probatus fuerit, accipiet coronam vitae ;* that is : " From that he have been proved, then shall he take the crown of life " ; [3] as who saith (according to mine understanding touched before) : But if a sinner have been proved before in divers temptations, now rising, now falling, falling by frailty, rising by grace, he shall never else take of God in this life ghostly wisdom in clear knowing of himself and of his inward dispositions, nor full discretion in counselling and teaching of others, nor yet the third, the which is the perfection of virtue in loving of his God and of his brethren. All these three— wisdom, discretion, and perfection of virtue—are but one, and they may be cleped the crown of life.

In a crown are three things : gold is the first ; precious stones are the second ; and the turrets of the flower-de-luce, raised up above the head, those are the third. By gold, wisdom ; by the precious stones, discretion ; and

---

[1] The MSS. usually read " cleped " for " called."
[2] Pepwell modernises to " trouble."   [3] Jas. i. 12.

by the turrets of the flower-de-luce, I understand the
perfection of virtue. Gold environeth the head, and
by wisdom we govern our ghostly work on every side ;
precious stones giveth light in beholding of men, and
by discretion we teach and counsel our brethren ; the
turrets of the flower-de-luce giveth two side branches,
spreading one to the right side and another to the left,
and one even up above the head, and by perfection of
virtues (the which is charity) we give two side branches
of love, the which are spreading, one to the right side to
our friends, and one to the left side to our enemies, and
one even up unto God, above man's understanding, the
which is the head of the soul. This is the crown of life
the which by grace may be gotten here in this life ; and,
therefore, bear thee low in thy battle, and suffer meekly
thy temptations till thou have been proved. For then
shalt thou take either the one crown, or the other, or
both, this here, and the other there ; for who so hath
this here, he may be full siker of the other there ; and full
many there are that are full graciously proved here, and
yet come never to this that may be had here in this life.
The which (if they meekly continue and patiently abide
the will of our Lord) shall full worthily and abundantly
receive the other there, in the high bliss of heaven. Thee
thinketh this crown fair that may be had here ; yea,
bear thee as meekly as thou mayst by grace, for in comparison of the other there, it is but as one noble to a

world full of gold. All this I say to give thee comfort
and evidence of strength in thy ghostly battle, the which
thou hast taken on hand in the trust of our Lord, and
all this I say to let thee see how far thou art yet from
the true knowing of thine inward disposition, and thereafter to give thee warning, not over soon to give stead [1]
nor to follow the singular stirrings of thy young heart,
for dread of deceit.

All this I say for to shew unto thee my conceit that I
have of thee and of thy stirrings, as thou hast asked of
me ; for I conceive of thee that thou art full able and
full greatly disposed to such sudden stirrings of singular
doings,[2] and full fast to cleave unto them when they be
received ; and that is full perilous. I say not that this
ableness and this greedy disposition in thee, or in any
other that is disposed as thou art, though all it be perilous,
that it is therefore evil in itself ; nay, so say I not, God
forbid that thou take it so ; but I say that it is full good
in itself, and a full great ableness to full great perfection,
yea, and to the greatest perfection that may be in this
life ; I mean, if that a soul that is so disposed will busily,
night and day, meek it [3] to God and to good counsel, and
strongly rise and martyr itself, with casting down of the
own wit and the own will in all such sudden and singular

---

[1] To give place to.
[2] Such impulses to exceptional practices.
[3] Humble itself.

stirrings, and say sharply that it will not follow such stirrings, seem they never so liking,[1] so high nor so holy, but if it have thereto the witness [2] and the consents of some ghostly teachers—I mean such as have been of long time expert in singular living. Such a soul, for ghostly continuance thus in this meekness, may deserve, through grace and the experience of this ghostly battle thus with itself, for to take the crown of life touched before. And as great an ableness to good as is this manner of disposition in a soul that is thus meeked as I say, as perilous it is in another soul, such one that will suddenly, without advisement of counsel, follow the stirrings of the greedy heart, by the own wit and the own will; and therefore, for God's love, beware with this ableness and with this manner of disposition (that I speak of), if it be in thee as I say. And meek thee continually to prayer and to counsel. Break down thine own wit and thy will in all such sudden and singular stirrings, and follow them not over lightly, till thou wete whence they come, and whether they be according for thee or not.

And as touching these stirrings of the which thou askest my conceit and my counsel, I say to thee that I conceive of them suspiciously, that is, that [3] they should be conceived on the ape's manner. Men say commonly that the ape doth as he seeth others do; forgive me if I err in my suspicion, I pray thee. Nevertheless, the love that

---

[1] Pleasant.   [2] Pepwell reads: "wits."   [3] Lest.

I have to thy soul stirreth me by evidence that I have of
a ghostly brother of thine and of mine, touched with
those same stirrings of full great [1] silence, of full singular
fasting, and of full only woning, on ape's manner, as he
granted unto me after long communing with me, and
when he had proved himself and his stirrings. For, as
he said, he had seen a man in your country, the which
man, as it is well known, is evermore in great silence, in
singular fasting, and in only dwelling; and certes, as I
suppose fully, they are full true stirrings those that that
man hath, caused all only of grace, that he feeleth by
experience within, and not of any sight or heard say that
he hath of any other man's silence without—the which
cause if it were, it should be cleped apely, as I say in my
simple meaning. And therefore beware, and prove well
thy stirrings, and whence they come; for how so thou art
stirred, whether from within by grace, or from without
on ape's manner, God wote, and I not. Nevertheless
this may I say thee in eschewing of perils like unto this:
look that thou be no ape, that is to say, look that thy
stirrings to silence or to speaking, to fasting or to eating,
to onliness or to company, whether they be come from
within of abundance of love and of devotion in the spirit,
and not from without by the windows of thy bodily wits,
as thine ears, and thine eyes. For, as Jeremiah saith
plainly, by such windows cometh in death: *Mors intrat*

[1] Pepwell reads: "strait."

per fenestras.[1] And this sufficeth, as little as it is, for answer to the first, where thou askest of me, what is my conceit of thee, and of these stirrings that thou speakest of to me in thy letter.

And touching the second thing, where thou askest of me my counsel in this case, and in such other when they fall, I beseech almighty Jesu (as He is cleped the angel of great counsel) that He of His mercy be thy counsellor and thy comforter in all thy noye and thy nede, and order me with His wisdom to fulfil in party by my teaching, so simple as it is, the trust of thine heart, the which thou hast unto me before many others—a simple lewd[2] wretch as I am, unworthy to teach thee or any other, for little-ness of grace and for lacking of conning. Nevertheless, though I be lewd, yet shall I somewhat say, answering to

---

[1] Jer. ix. 21: "Quia ascendit mors per fenestras nostras" (Vulgate). Pepwell reads: "as saint Jerome saith"! Cf. Walter Hilton, *The Ladder of Perfection*, I. pt. iii. cap. 9: "Lift up thy lanthorn, and thou shalt see in this image five windows, by which sin cometh into thy soul, as the Prophet saith: *Death cometh in by our windows.* These are the five senses by which thy soul goeth out of herself, and fetcheth her delight, and seeketh her feeding in earthly things, contrary to the nobility of her own nature. As by the eye to see curious and fair things, and so of the other senses. By the unskilful using of these senses willingly to vanities, thy soul is much letted from the sweetness of the spiritual senses within; and therefore it behoveth thee to stop these windows, and shut them, but only when need requireth to open them" (ed. Dalgairns, p. 115).

[2] Ignorant.

thy desire at my simple conning, with a trust in God that
His grace shall be learner and leader when conning of
kind and of clergy defaileth.[1] Thou wotest right well
thyself that silence in itself nor speaking, also singular
fasting nor common dieting, onliness nor company, all
these nor yet any of them be not the true end of our
desire ; but to some men (and not to all) they are means
helping to the end, if they be done lawfully and with
discretion, and else are they more letting than furthering.
And therefore plainly [2] to speak, nor plainly to be still,
plainly to eat, nor plainly to fast, plainly to be in company, or plainly to be only, think I not to counsel thee
at this time ; for why, perfection standeth not in them.
But this counsel may I give thee generally, to hold thee
by in these stirrings, and in all other like unto these ;
evermore where thou findest two contraries, as are these
—silence and speaking, fasting and eating, onliness and
company, common clothing of Christian religion and
singular habits of divers and devised brotherhoods, with
all such other what so they be, the which in themself are
but works of kind [3] and of men. For thou hast it by kind
and by statute of thine outer man now for to speak and
now for to be still, now for to eat and now for to fast,
now for to be in company and now to be only, now to be
common in clothing and now to be in singular habit,

[1] Where natural and acquired knowledge alike fall short.
[2] Fully.   [3] Nature.

ever when thee list, and when thou seest [1] that any of them should be speedful and helply to thee in nourishing of the heavenly grace working within in thy soul; but if it be so (which God forbid), that thou or any other be so lewd and so blinded in the sorrowful temptations of the midday devil, that ye bind you by any crooked avow to any such singularities, as it were under colour of holiness feigned under such an holy thraldom,[2] in full and final destroying of the freedom of Christ, the which is the ghostly habit of the sovereign holiness that may be in this life, or in the other, by the witness of saint Paul saying thus: *Ubi spiritus Domini, ibi libertas:* "There where the spirit of God is, there is freedom." [3] And thereto when thou seest that all such works in their use may be both good and evil; I pray thee leave them both, for that is the most ease for thee for to do, if thou wilt be meek, and leave the curious beholding and seeking in thy wits to look whether is better. But do thou thus: set the one on the one hand, and the other on the other, and choose thee a thing the which is hid between them; the which thing, when it is had, giveth thee leave in freedom of spirit to begin and to cease in holding any of the others at thine own full list, without any blame.

But now thou askest me, what is that thing. I shall

---

[1] Pepwell has: "when thou dost feel."

[2] Pepwell inserts: "I mean except the solemn vows of holy religion."   [3] 2 Cor. iii. 17.

.ell thee what I mean that it is : *It is God ;* for whom
thou shouldest be still, if thou shouldest be still ; and
for whom thou shouldest speak, if thou shouldest speak ;
and for whom thou shouldest fast, if thou shouldest fast ;
and for whom thou shouldest eat, if thou shouldest eat ;
and for whom thou shouldest be only, if thou shouldest
be only ; and for whom thou shouldest be in company,
if thou shouldest be in company. And so forth of all
the remenant, what so they be. For silence is not God,
nor speaking is not God ; fasting is not God, nor eating
is not God ; onliness is not God, nor company is not
God ; nor yet any of all the other such two contraries.
He is hid between them, and may not be found by any
work of thy soul, but all only by love of thine heart. He
may not be known by reason, He may not be gotten by
thought, nor concluded by understanding ; but He may
be loved and chosen with the true lovely will of thine
heart.[1]   Choose thee Him, and thou art silently speaking,

---

[1] Cf. St. Catherine of Siena, Letter 308 (ed. Gigli) : "Love
harmonises the three powers of our soul, and binds them together.
The will moves the understanding to see, when it wishes to love ;
when the understanding perceives that the will would fain love, if
it is a rational will, it places before it as object the ineffable love of
the eternal Father, who has given us the Word, His own Son, and
the obedience and humility of the Son, who endured torments, in-
uries, mockeries, and insults with meekness and with such great
love. And thus the will, with ineffable love, follows what the eye
of the understanding has beheld ; and, with its strong hand, it
stores up in the memory the treasure that it draws from this love."

and speakingly silent, fastingly eating, and eatingly fasting, and so forth of all the remenant. Such a lovely
choosing of God, thus wisely lesinge [1] and seeking Him
out with the true will of a clean heart, between all such
two leaving them both, when they come and proffer them
to be the point and the prick of our ghostly beholding,
is the worthiest tracing and seeking of God that may
be gotten or learned in this life. I mean for a soul that
will be contemplative ; yea, though all that a soul that
thus seeketh see nothing that may be conceived with the
ghostly eye of reason ; for if God be thy love and thy
meaning, the choice and the point of thine heart, it
sufficeth to thee in this life (though all thou see never
more of Him with the eyes of thy reason all thy life time).
Such a blind shot with the sharp dart of longing love
may never fail of the prick, the which is God, as Himself
saith in the book of love, where He speaketh to a lan-
guishing soul and a loving, saying thus : *Vulnerasti cor
meum, soror mea, amica mea, et sponsa mea, vulnerasti cor
meum, in uno oculorum tuorum :* "Thou hast wounded
mine heart, my sister, my leman, and my spouse, thou
hast wounded mine heart in one of thine eyes." [2] Eyes
of the soul they are two : Reason and Love. By reason
we may trace how mighty, how wise, and how good He
is in His creatures, but not in Himself ; but ever when
reason defaileth, then list, love, live and learn, to play,[3]

[1] Losing.   [2] Cant. iv. 9.   [3] To exercise love.

for by love we may feel Him, find Him, and hit Him,
even in Himself.   It is a wonderful eye, this love, for of
a loving soul it is only said of our Lord : " Thou hast
wounded mine heart in one of thine eyes " ; that is to
say, in love that is blind to many things, and seeth but
that one thing that it seeketh, and therefore it findeth
and feeleth, hitteth and woundeth the point and the
prick that it shooteth at, well sooner than it should if the
sight were sundry in beholding of many things, as it is
when the reason ransacketh and seeketh among all such
sere [1] things as are these : silence and speaking, singular
fasting and common eating, onliness or company, and all
such other ; to look whether is better.

Let be this manner of doing, I pray thee, and let as
thou wist not that there were any such means (I mean
ordained for to get God by) ; for truly no more there is,
if thou wilt be very contemplative and soon sped of thy
purpose.   And, therefore, I pray thee and other like unto
thee, with the Apostle saying thus : *Videte vocationem
vestram, et in ea vocatione qua vocati estis state :* [2] " See
your calling, and, in that calling that ye be called, stand
stiffly and abide in the name of Jesu."   Thy calling
is to be very contemplative, ensampled by Mary Magdalene.   Do then as Mary did, set the point of thine
heart upon one thing : *Porro unum est necessarium :* " For

1 Divers.
2 1 Cor. i. 26, vii. 20 ; Eph. iv. 1.

one thing is necessary," [1] the which is God. Him wouldest
thou have, Him seekest thou, Him list thee to love, Him
list thee to feel,[2] Him list thee hold thee by, and neither
by silence nor by speaking, by singular fasting nor by
common eating, by onliness nor by companious woning,
by hard wearing nor by easy ; for sometime silence is
good, but that same time speaking were better ; and
againward sometime speaking is good, but that same time
silence were better ; and so forth of all the remenant,
as is fasting, eating, onliness, and company ; for sometime the one is good, but the other is better, but neither
of them is at any time the best.   And, therefore, let be
good all that is good, and better all that is better,[3] for
both they will defail and have an end ; and choose thee
the best with Mary, thy mirror, that never will defail :
*Maria (inquit optimus) optimam partem elegit, quae non
auferetur ab ea.*[4] The best is almighty Jesu, and He said
that Mary, in ensample of all contemplatives, had chosen
the best, the which should never be taken from her ; and
therefore, I pray thee, with Mary leave the good and the
better, and choose thee the best.

Let them be, all such things as are these : silence and
speaking, fasting and eating, onliness and company, and

[1] Luke x. 42.

[2] Pepwell inserts : "Him list thee to see, and."

[3] Pepwell reads : "Let be good and all that is good, and better
with all that is better."

[4] Luke x. 42.

all such other, and take no keep to them ; thou wotest
not what they mean, and, I pray thee, covet not to wit ;
and if thou shall at any time think or speak of them, think
then and say that they are so high and so worthy things of
perfection, for to conne[1] speak, or for to conne be still,
for to conne fast, and for to conne eat, for to conne be
only, and to conne be in company, that it were but a
folly and a foul presumption to such a frail wretch as
thou art, for to meddle thee of so great perfection.   For
why, for to speak, and for to be still, for to eat, and for
to fast, for to be only, and for to be in company, ever
when we will, may we have by kind ; but for to conne do
all these, we may not but by grace.   And, without doubt,
such grace is never gotten by any mean of such strait
silence, of such singular fasting, or of such only dwelling
that thou speakest of, the which is caused from without
by occasion of hearing and of seeing of any other man's
such singular doings.   But if ever this grace shall be
gotten, it behoveth to be learned of God from within,
unto whom thou hast listily leaned many a day before
with all the love of thine heart, utterly voiding from
thy ghostly beholding[2] all manner of sight of any thing
beneath Him ; though all that some of those things that
I bid thee thus void, should seem in the sight of some
men a full worthy mean to get God by.   Yea, say what

[1] To know how to speak, etc.
[2] Banishing from thy soul's vision.

men say will, but do thou as I say thee, and let the proof witness.   For to him that will be soon sped of his purpose ghostly, it sufficeth to him for a mean, and him needeth no more, but the actual mind of good God only, with a reverent stirring of lasting love ; so that mean unto God gettest thou none but God.   If thou keep whole thy stirring of love that thou mayst feel by grace in thine heart, and scatter not thy ghostly beholding therefrom, then that same that thou feelest shall well conne [1] tell thee when thou shalt speak and when thou shalt be still, and it shall govern thee discreetly in all thy living without any error, and teach thee mistily [2] how thou shalt begin and cease in all such doing of kind with a great and sovereign discretion.   For if thou mayst by grace keep it in custom and in continual working, then, if it be needful or speedful to thee for to speak, for to commonly eat, or for to bide in company, or for to do any such other thing that longeth to the common true custom of Christian men, and of kind, it shall first stir thee full softly to speak or to do that other common thing of kind, what so it be. And then, if thou do it not, it shall strike as sore as a prick on thine heart and pain thee full sore, and let thee have no peace [3] but if thou do it.   And, on the same

[1] Be able to.

[2] Pepwell reads : " privily."   Cf. Wyclif (Select English Works, ed. cit., i. p. 149): "And after seith Crist to his apostles, *that thes thingis he seide bifore to hem in proverbis* and mystily."

[3] Pepwell reads : "rest."

manner, if thou be in speaking, or in any such other work
that is common to the course of kind, if it be needful and
speedful to thee to be still, and for to set thee to the
contrary, as is onliness to company, fasting to eating, and
all such other the which are works of singular holiness,
it will stir thee to them ; so that thus, by experience of
such a blind stirring of love unto God, a contemplative
soul cometh sooner to that grace of discretion for to conne
speak, and for to conne be still, for to conne eat, and for
to conne fast, for to conne be in company, and for to
conne be only,[1] and all such other, than by any such
singularities as thou speakest of, taken by the stirrings of
man's own wit and his will within in himself, or yet by
the ensample of any other man's doing without, what so
it be. For why, such strained doings under the stirrings
of kind, without touching [2] of grace, is a passing pain
without any profit ; but if it be to them that are religious,
or that have them by enjoining of penance, where profit
riseth only because of obedience, and not by any such
straitness of doing without ; the which is painful to all
that it proveth. But lovely and listily to will to love [3]
God is great and passing ease, true ghostly peace, and

---

[1] Pepwell modernises "conne" to "learn to" throughout this passage.
[2] Harl. MS. 674 reads : "stirring"; the other MS. as Pepwell.
[3] Harl. MS. 674 reads : "have."

earnest of the endless rest. And, therefore, speak when thee list, and leave when thee list, eat when thee list, and fast when thee list, be in company when thee list, and be by thyself when thee list, so that [1] God and grace be thy leader. Let fast who fast will, and be only who will, and let hold silence who so will, but hold thee by God that doth beguile no man ; for silence and speaking, onliness and company, fasting and eating, all may beguile thee. And if thou hear of any man that speaketh, or of any that is still, of any that eateth or of any that fasteth, or of any that is in company or else by himself, think thou, and say, if thee list, that they conne do as they should do, but if the contrary shew in apert.[2] But look that thou do not as they do (I mean for that they do so) on ape's manner ; for neither thou canst, nor peradventure thou art not disposed as they are. And, therefore, leave to work after other men's dispositions, and work after thine own, if thou mayst know what it is. And unto the time that thou mayst know what it is, work after those men's counsel that know their own disposition, but not after their disposition ;[3] for such men should

---

[1] Pepwell reads : "else."

[2] Manifestly, *i.e.* unless they clearly show that they do not know how to act as they should. Pepwell has : " in a part."

[3] *i.e.* take their advice, but do not simply imitate them. I follow the MSS. in preference to Pepwell, who reads : "Work after no men's counsel, but sith that know well their own disposition ; for such men should," etc.

give counsel in such cases, and else none. And this sufficeth for an answer to all thy letter, as me thinketh ; the grace of God be ever more with thee, in the name of Jesu. AMEN.

FINIT EPISTOLA

VII

HERE FOLLOWETH A DEVOUT TREATISE OF
DISCERNING OF SPIRITS, VERY NECESSARY
FOR GHOSTLY LIVERS

HERE FOLLOWETH A DEVOUT TREATISE OF DISCERNING OF SPIRITS, VERY NECESSARY FOR GHOSTLY LIVERS

FOR because that there be divers kinds of spirits, therefore it is needful to us discreet knowing of them; sith it so is that we be taught of the apostle saint John not to believe to all spirits.[1] For it might seem to some that are but little in conning, and namely of ghostly things, that each thought that soundeth in man's heart should be the speech of none other spirit but only of man's own spirit. And that it is not so, both belief and witness of holy scripture proveth apertly; for " I shall hear," saith the prophet David, " not what I speak myself, but what my Lord God speaketh in me " ; [2] and another prophet saith, that an angel spake in him.[3] And also we be taught in the psalm that the wicked spirits sendeth evil thoughts in to men ; and over this, that there is a spirit of the flesh not good, the apostle Paul sheweth apertly, where he saith, that some men are full blown or inflate with the spirit of their flesh.[4] And also that there is the spirit

[1] 1 John iv. 1–6.   [2] Ps. lxxxv. 8 (Vulgate lxxxiv. 9).
[3] Zech. i. 9–19.   [4] Col. ii. 18.

of the world, he declareth plainly, where he maketh joy
in God, not only for himself, but also for his disciples,
that they had not taken that spirit of the world, but that
that is sent of God, the which is the Holy Ghost.[1] And
these two spirits of the flesh and also of the world are, as
it were, servants or sergeants of that cursed spirit, the
foul fiend of hell; so that the spirit of wickedness is lord
of the spirit of the flesh, and also of the spirit of the world.
And which of these three spirits that speaketh to our
spirit, we should not believe them. For why, they
speak never but that anon, by their speaking, they lead to
the loss both of body and of soul. And which spirit it is
that speaketh to our spirit, the speech of that same spirit
that speaketh shall fully declare; for ever more the spirit
of the flesh speaketh soft things and easy to the body;
the spirit of the world vain things and covetise [2] of worship; and the spirit of malice of the fiend speaketh fell
things and bitter.

Wherefore, as oft times as any thought smiteth on our
hearts of meat, of drink, and of sleep, of soft clothing, of
lechery, and of all other such things the which longeth to
the business of the flesh, and maketh our heart for to
brenne [3] as it were in a longing desire after all such things;

---

[1] 1 Thess. i. 2–9.
[2] Pepwell adds: "or ambition." Cf. Chaucer, *The Persones
Tale*, ed. Skeat, § 18: "and coveitise of hynesse by pryde of
herte."   [3] Burn.

be we full siker that it is the spirit of the flesh that speaketh
it.   And therefore put we him away, in as much as we
goodly may by grace, for he is our adversary.   As oft
times as any thought smiteth on our hearts of vain joy
of this world, kindling in us a desire to be holden fair,
and to be favoured, to be holden of great kin and of great
conning, to be holden wise and worthy, or else to have
great degree and high office in this life—such thoughts
and all other the which would make a man to seem high
and worshipful, not only in the sight of others, but also
in the sight of himself—no doubt but it is the spirit of the
world that speaketh all these, a far more perilous enemy
than is the spirit of the flesh, and with much more business he should be put off.   And oft times it befalleth that
these two servants and sergeants of the foul fiend, the
spirit and prince of wrath [1] and of wickedness, are either
by grace and by ghostly slight of a soul stiffly put down
and trodden down under foot ; or else, by quaintise [2] of
their malicious master, the foul fiend of hell, they are
quaintly withdrawn, for he thinketh himself for to rise
with great malice and wrath, as a lion running felly to
assail the sickness of our sely souls ; and this befalleth as
oft as the thought of our heart stirreth us, not to the lust
of our flesh, nor yet to the vain joy of this world, but it
stirreth us to murmuring, to grutching,[3] to grievance, and

[1] So Harl. MS. 674 ; Pepwell has : " war."
[2] Crafty device.   [3] Cf. above, p. 17 note.

to bitterness of soul, to pain and to impatience, to wrath, to melancholy, and to evil will, to hate, to envy, and to all such sorrows. It maketh us to bear us heavily, if ought be done or said unto us, not so lovely, nor so wisely [1] as we would it were ; it raiseth in us all evil suspicion, if ought be shewed in sign, in countenance, in word, or in work, that might by any manner be turned to malice or to heaviness of heart ; it maketh us as fast [2] to take it to us.

To these thoughts, and to all such that would put us out of peace and restfulness of heart, we should none otherwise againstand,[3] but as we would the self fiend of hell, and as much we should flee therefrom as from the loss of our soul. No doubt but both the other two thoughts, of the spirit of the flesh and also of the spirit of the world, work and travail in all that they can to the loss of our soul, but most perilously the spirit of malice ; for why, he is by himself, but they not without him. For if a man's soul be never so clean of fleshly lust, and of vain joy of this world, and if it be defouled with this spirit of malice, of wrath, and of wickedness, not againstanding all the other cleanness before, yet it is losable. And if a soul be never so much defouled with the lust of the flesh, and vain joy of the world, and it may by grace keep it in peace and in restfulness of heart unto the

[1] Pepwell has : " gladly."
[2] Pepwell reads : " ever ready."
[3] Withstand, resist.

even Christian,[1] though all it be full hard for to do (lasting the custom of the other two),[2] yet it is less losable, not againstanding all the other filth of the flesh and of the world touched before. And, therefore, though all that our lusty [3] thoughts of our flesh be evil, for they reave from the soul the life of devotion, and though all that the vain joy of the world be worse, for it reaveth us from the true joy that we should have in contemplation of heavenly things, ministered and taught to us by the angels of heaven. For who so lustily desireth to be worshipped, favoured, and served of men here in earth, they deserve to forego the worship, the favour, and service of angel in ghostly contemplation of heaven and of heavenly things, all their lifetime ; the which contemplation is better and more worthy in itself than is the lust and the liking of devotion. And for this bitterness I clepe the spirit of malice, of wrath, and of wickedness the worst spirit of them all ; and why ? Certes, for it reaveth us the best thing of all, and that is charity, the which is God. For who so lacketh peace and restfulness of heart, him lacketh the lively presence of the lovely sight of the high peace of heaven, good gracious God His own dear self. This witnesseth David in the psalm,

---

[1] Cf. Mother Juliana, *Revelations of Divine Love*, i. cap. 9 : " In general I am, I hope, in onehead of charity with all my even Christian; for in this onehead standeth the life of all mankind that shall be saved."   [2] If it is still guilty of the other two.

[3] Pepwell adds : " and voluptuous."

where he saith, that the place of God is made in peace, and His dwelling place in Sion.[1] Sion is as much to say as the sight of peace ; the sight of the soul is the thought of that same soul ; and, certes, in that soul that most is occupied in thoughts of peace hath God made His dwelling place.[2] And thus saith Himself by the prophet, when he saith : " Upon whom shall my spirit rest, but upon the meek and the restful." [3] And, therefore, who so will have God continually dwelling in him, and live in love and in sight of the high peace of the Godhead, the which is the highest and the best party of contemplation that may be had in this life, be he busy night and day to put down, when they come, the spirit of the flesh and the spirit of the world, but most busily the spirit of malice, of wrath, and of wickedness, for he is the foulest and the worst filth [4] of all. And it is full needful and speedful to know his quaintise, and not for to unknow his doleful deceits. For sometime he will, that wicked cursed wight, change his likeness in to an angel of light, that he may under colour of virtue do more dere ; [5] but

[1] Ps. cxxxii. (Vulgate cxxxi.) 13.

[2] Cf. Walter Hilton, *The Ladder of Perfection*, II. pt. ii. cap. 3 : "*Jerusalem* is, as much as to say, *a sight of peace ;* and betokeneth contemplation in perfect love of God ; for contemplation is nothing else but a sight of God, which is very peace."

[3] Probably Isa. lvii. 15.   [4] Pepwell reads : " most folly."

[5] Pepwell adds : " or harm." Cf. *The Chronicle of Robert of Brunne*, 8905–6 : " Now may ye lyghtly bere the stones to schip wythouten dere.'

yet then, if we look more redely,[1] it is but seed of bitterness and of discord that that he sheweth, seem it never so holy nor never so fair at the first shewing.   Full many he stirreth unto singular holiness passing the common statute and custom of their degree, as is fasting, sharp wearing, and many other devout observances and outward doings, in open reproving of other men's defaults, the which they have not of office for to do.   All such and many other he stirreth them for to do, and all under colour of devotion and of charity ; not for he is delighted in any deed of devotion and of charity, but for he loveth dissension and slander, the which is evermore caused by such unseemly singularities ; for where so ever that any one or two are in any devout congregation, the which any one or two useth any such outward singularities, then in the sight of fools all the remenant are slandered by them ; but, in the sight of the wise man, they slander themselves.   But for because that fools are more than wise men, therefore for favour of fools such singular doers ween that they be wise, when (if it were wisely determined) they and all their fautors [2] should be seen apert fools, and darts shot of the devil, to slay true simple souls under colour of holiness and charity.   And thus many deceits can the fiend bring in on this manner.

Who so will not consent, but meeketh him truly to prayer and to counsel, shall graciously be delivered of all

[1] Advisedly.   [2] Partisans, abettors.

these deceits.[1]   But it is sorrow for to say, and more for to feel, that sometime [2] our own spirit is so overcome peradventure with each of these three spirits, of the flesh, of the world, and of the fiend, and so brought into danger, bounden in bondage, in thraldom and in service of them all, that sorrow it is to wit.   In great confusion and loss of itself, it doth now the office of each one of them itself in itself.   And this befalleth when, after long use, and customable consenting unto them when they come, at the last it is made so fleshly, so worldly, and so malicious, so wicked, and so froward, that now plainly of itself, without suggestion of any other spirit, it gendereth and bringeth forth in itself, not only lusty thoughts of the flesh, and vain thoughts of the world, but that worst of all these, as are bitter thoughts and wicked, in backbiting, and deeming, and evil suspicion of others.   And when it is thus with our spirit, then, I trow, it may not lightly be known when it is our own spirit that speaketh, or when it heareth any of the other three spirits speaking in it, as it is touched before.   But what maketh it matter [3] who speaketh, when it is all one and the same thing that is spoken ?   What helpeth to know the person of him that speaketh, when it is siker and certain that all is evil

[1] The MSS. read : " doles."

[2] Pepwell reads : " But it is more sorrow to feel of our own spirit's deceits.   For sometime our own spirit."

[3] The MSS. read : " Bot what thar reche " ; what need to care.

and perilous that is spoken ? If it be thine enemy, consent not to him, but meek thee to prayer and to counsel, and so mayst thou mightily withstand thine enemy. If it be thine own spirit, reprove him bitterly, and sighingly sorrow that ever thou fell in [1] so great wretchedness, bondage, and thraldom of the devil. Shrive thee of thy customed consents, and of thine old sins, and so mayst thou come (by grace) to recover thy freedom again ; and by the gracious freedom mayst thou soon come to, wisely for to know, and soothfastly for to feel by the proof, when it is thine own spirit that speaketh these evils, or it be these other evil spirits that speaketh them in thee. And so may this knowing be a sovereign mean and help of againstanding, for often times unknowing is cause of much error, and, againward, knowing is cause of much truth ; and to this manner of knowing mayst thou win thus as I say to thee.

If thou be in doubt or in were [2] of these evil thoughts when they come, whether that they be the speech of thine own spirit, or of any of the others of thine enemies ; look then busily by the witness of thy counsel and thy conscience, if thou have been shriven and lawfully amended after the doom [3] of thy confessor, of all the consents that ever thou consented to that kind of sin, that thy

[1] Pepwell reads : " didst feel in thee."
[2] Cf. above, p. 95 note.
[3] Pepwell adds : " and judgment.

thought is aware of.   And if thou have not been shriven, shrive thee then, as truly as thou mayst, by grace and by counsel; and then wete thou right well that all the thoughts that come to thee after thy shrift, stirring thee oft times to the same sins, they are the words of other spirits than thine own (I mean some of the three touched before).   And thou for none such thoughts, be they never so thick, so foul, nor so many (I mean for their first coming in), but if it be for recklessness of again-standing,[1] art no blame worthy.   And not only releasing of purgatory that thou hast deserved for the same sins done before, what so they be, thou mayst deserve, if thou stiffly againstand them, but also much grace in this life, and much meed in the bliss of heaven.   But all those evil thoughts coming in to thee, stirring thee to any sin, after that thou hast consented to that same sin, and before that thou hast sorrow for that consent, and art in will to be shriven thereof, it is no peril to thee to take them to thyself,[2] and for to shrive thee of them, as of thoughts of thine own spirit; but for to take to thyself all other thoughts, the which thou hast by very proof, as it is shewed before, by the speeches of other spirits than of thyself, therein lieth great peril, for so mightest thou lightly misrule thy conscience, charging a thing

---

[1] Unless because of carelessness in resisting them when they first come.

[2] To regard thyself as responsible.

for sin the which is none ; and this were great error, and
a mean to the greatest peril. For if it were so that each
evil thought and stirring to sin were the work and the
speech of none other spirit, but only of man's own spirit ;
then it would follow by that that a man's own spirit were
a very fiend, the which is apertly false and a damnable
woodness ;[1] for though all it be so that a soul may, by
frailty and custom of sinning, fall in to so much wretchedness, that it taketh on itself by bondage of sin the office
of the devil, stirring itself to sin ever more and more,
without any suggestion of any other spirit (as it is said
before), yet it is not therefore a devil in kind, but it is
a devil in office, and may be cleped devilish, for it is in
the doing like to the devil, [that is to say, a stirrer of itself
unto sin, the which is the office of the devil].[2] Nevertheless yet, for all this thraldom to sin and devilishness
in office, it may by grace of contrition, of shrift, and of
amending, recover the freedom again, and be made save-
able—yea, and a full special God's saint in this life, that
before was full damnable and full cursed in the living.[3]
And, therefore, as great a peril as it is a soul that is fallen
in sin, not for to charge his conscience therewith, nor for
to amend him thereof, as great a peril it is, and, if it may

[1] Madness.
[2] Not in Harl. MS. 674.
[3] Pepwell reads : " a full damnable and a full cursed fiend in
his living."

be said, a greater, a man for to charge his conscience with each thought and stirring of sin that will come in him ; for, by such nice charging of conscience, might he lightly run in to error of conscience, and so be led in to despair all his life time. And the cause of all this is lacking of knowing of discretion of spirits, the which knowing may be gotten by very experience ; who so redely will look soon after that a soul have been truly cleansed by confession, as it is said before. For fast after confession a soul is, as it were, a clean paper leaf, for ableness that it hath to receive what that men will write thereupon. Both they do press [1] for to write on the soul, when it is clean in itself made by confession : God and His angel on the one party, and the fiend and his angel on the other party ; but it is in the free choice of the soul to receive which that it will. The receipt of the soul is the consent of the same soul. A new thought and a stirring to any sin, the which thou hast forsaken before in thy shrift, what is it else but the speech of one of the three spirits the which are thine enemies (touched before), proffering to write on thy soul the same sin again ? The speech of thyself, is it not ; for why, there is no such thing written in thy soul, for all it is wasted away before in thy shrift, and thy soul left naked and bare ; nothing left thereupon, but a frail and a free consent, more inclining to the evil, for custom therein, than it is to the good, but more able to the good

[1] Pepwell adds : " and desire much."

than to the evil, for cleanness of the soul and virtue of the sacrament of shrift ; but, of itself, it hath nought then, where through it may think or stir itself to good or to evil ; and, therefore, it followeth that what thought that cometh then in it, whether that it be good or evil, it is not of itself, but the consent to the good or to the evil, whether that it be, that is ever more the work of the same soul.

And all after the worthiness and the wretchedness of this consent, thereafter it deserveth pain or bliss. If this consent be to evil, then as fast it hath, by cumbrance of sin, the office of that same spirit that first made him suggestion of that same sin ; and if it be to the good, then as fast it hath, by grace, the office of that same spirit that first made him stirring [1] to that same good. For as oft as any healful thought cometh in our mind, as of chastity, of soberness, of despising of the world, of wilful poverty, of patience, of meekness, and of charity, without doubt it is the spirit of God that speaketh, either by Himself or else by some of His angels—that is to say, either His angels of this life, the which are true teachers, or else His angels of His bliss, the which are true stirrers and inspirers of good. And as it is said of the other three evil spirits, that a soul, for long use and customable consenting unto them, may be made so fleshly, so worldly, and so malicious, that it taketh upon it the office of them

[1] Pepwell reads : "suggestion."

aal; right so it is againward[1] that a soul, for long use and custom in goodness, may be made so ghostly by cleanness of living and devotion of spirit against the spirit of the flesh, and so heavenly against the spirit of the world, and so godly by peace and by charity, and by restfulness of heart, against the spirit of malice, of wrath, and of wickedness, that it hath them now of office all such good thoughts to think when him list, without forgetting, in as great perfection as the frailty of this life will suffer. And thus it may be seen how that each thought that smiteth on our hearts, whether that it be good or evil, it is not evermore the speech of our own spirit, but the consent to the thought, what so ever it be, that is ever of our own spirit. Jesu grant us His grace, to consent to the good and againstand the evil. AMEN.

[1] On the other hand.

FINIS.   DEO GRATIAS

INDEX OF
NAMES & SCRIPTURAL REFERENCES